Opa!

Stories and

Traditions of a

Greek-American

Family

ARTHUR C. COSMAS, PhD

RIVER GROVE
BOOKS

This publication is designed to provide accurate and authoritative information in regard to the subject matter covered. It is sold with the understanding that the publisher and author are not engaged in rendering legal, accounting, or other professional services. If legal advice or other expert assistance is required, the services of a competent professional should be sought.

Published by River Grove Books
Austin, TX
www.rivergrovebooks.com

Copyright ©2018 Arthur Cosmas

All rights reserved.

Thank you for purchasing an authorized edition of this book and for complying with copyright law. No part of this book may be reproduced, stored in a retrieval system, or transmitted by any means, electronic, mechanical, photocopying, recording, or otherwise, without written permission from the copyright holder.

Distributed by River Grove Books

Design and composition by Greenleaf Book Group
Cover design by Greenleaf Book Group

Cataloging-in-Publication data is available.

Print ISBN: 978-1-63299-197-3

eBook ISBN: 978-1-63299-198-0

First Edition

Dedication

SHE WOULD SCRAPE STRAY CRUMBS *of bread and arrange them into neat little mounds on the kitchen table before she placed them into a napkin with her palm. She tore small pieces from the ends of a paper napkin and twisted the corners into tortured points before placing them neatly in little piles on the table.*

I remember repeatedly observing my mother as she nervously manipulated these objects whenever she sat at the table during the twilight of her life. Despite my concerns, and for reasons that apparently remain suppressed in my subconscious, I carefully preserved these actions in the notes section of my cell phone, where they remained latent and undeveloped for many months. Perhaps my mother's restless behavior was her way of provoking me to write about my Greek heritage, which would provide my grandchildren with an account of what it was like to be brought up as a Greek American, as well as to give them a written legacy about my life as a Greek American. Alternatively, it may have been the Greek gods commanding me to record these experiences for all of us to enjoy. Regardless of the reason, my wife, Pam, provided me with the incentive to write *Opa!* After several years of encouraging me to write a textbook, she finally suggested that I should write a book about Greek Americans, which is the book you're reading now.

And so, from those brief observations of my mother's anxiety-driven behavior that were saved in my cell phone and through the continuous encouragement of my wife, who had more confidence in me than I had in myself, I began writing this book. It is dedicated to her. If not for her reassurance, I would have given up, and *Opa!* would never have been completed.

This book is also written to provide my daughter, Samantha, and my grandchildren, Gabriel and Alexsandria, with a tangible memory of their father and grandfather, and I hope they will enjoy reading about what it was like being brought up as a Greek American in my generation.

Make no mistake about it.
We are Greeks, and the blood of ancient Greek heroes runs through our veins!

Πληρης καθαροαιμος Ελληνας
(full-blooded Greek)

Contents

PREFACE	ix
AUTHOR'S NOTE	xi
ACKNOWLEDGMENTS	xiii
INTRODUCTION	1

Part I: Being Greek

1	Greekness	7
2	Passion	21
3	Chaos	31

Part II: The Greek Community

4	The Agora	41
5	Family	51
6	Growing Up Greek	83

Part III: Culture and Tradition

7	The Greek Diet	109
8	Homeopathic Medicine and Superstition	127
9	Religious Holidays and Events	149

CONCLUSION: Assimilation and My Greek Legacy	169
EPILOGUE: It Is the Will of the Gods: I'm Coming Home, Dad	185
QUESTIONS FOR DISCUSSION	199
AUTHOR Q&A	201
GLOSSARY	207
ABOUT THE AUTHOR	211

Preface

THIS BOOK IS A DEPICTION of what it was like to be brought up as a Greek American in the 1950s. Filled with true-life anecdotes, it is an engaging and lovable portrayal of Greeks and Greek culture. The facts and descriptions throughout the book will interest readers who are *Hellinophiles* (a person who has a love of Greece and Greek culture). If you are Greek, these stories may revive tender memories and make you proud of your Greekness. If you are not Greek, these stories may remind you of what it was like for you growing up and give you an opportunity to learn quite a bit about Greek culture and traditions.

When I was young, most aspects of my life were Greek. As I wrote about my experiences, a constellation of poignant memories emerged. Because many of you have never been exposed to these unique Greek cultural traditions, I hope *Opa!* will provide you with insight as to what it was like for me and others of my generation to grow up as Greek Americans and that you will acquire a sense of what it means to be Greek.

We all have similar wants, needs, and concerns. We all laugh, we cry, we feel physical and emotional pain, we all want to feel important, and we all want something better for our children. Even though our cultures are different, when we interact with someone on an individual level, we are able to experience our similarities and our differences, which is an important social dynamic. A greater understanding of our cultural differences can enable us all to develop more acceptance and compassion for others.

I present these stories to you for your enjoyment and to remind both my Greek and non-Greek readers that we are a lot more alike than we are different (ειμαστε περισσοτερο απο οσο ειμαστε διαφορετικοι).

I hope you will enjoy reading this book as much as I enjoyed writing it.

Author's Note

THE TILE WAVE MOSAIC ON a beautiful Greek blue palette and the classic Greek key motif that appear on the cover are both symbols of the eternal flow of things. They also symbolize the bonds of friendship, love, and devotion.

Acknowledgments

I WOULD LIKE TO ACKNOWLEDGE the gracious attitude and tireless efforts of Daniel Eichner, Perry Siegel, and Joy Sanzo, who consistently provided technical assistance, without which this manuscript would not have been completed. I extend my acknowledgment and grateful appreciation to the Greenleaf Book Group staff, who encouraged and guided me through the development of *Opa!* Special gratitude to Lindsey Clark, lead editor, who had the enormous task of taking a collection of chaotic Greek stories and molding them into an entertaining narrative. Her efforts in the development of *Opa!* were immeasurable. Grateful recognition is given to the efforts of Elizabeth Chenette, who completed the detailed and comprehensive edit on this book, and to Pam Nordberg, who completed the proofread. Acknowledgment is also extended to Claire Jentsch, who encouraged me to submit excerpts of *Opa!* to Justin Branch and his team, who evaluated and accepted it, and to Rachael Brandenburg and her team for developing the cover design. Grateful appreciation is also extended to Jen Glynn, senior project manager, for her encouragement and for guiding the development of the book. And of course, acknowledgment and gratitude to my wife, Pam, my daughter, Samantha, and my son-in-law, Peter, who not only encouraged me but also tolerated my chaos as I wrote this story. I extend my love to my grandchildren, Gabriel and Alexsandria, who on several occasions asked me, "Papa, is your book going to be in the library?" And finally, my respect to the Greek gods who directed my life, for if I had to repeat it, most assuredly, they would choose the same path for me again!

Introduction

HAVE YOU EVER TRIED TO make sense of what your grandmother was saying? Did you ever feel, while talking with her, that nothing made any sense and you were losing your mind, and although she emphatically said the same thing repeatedly, nothing related to reality? Eventually, did you give up and walk away, dumbfounded?

Did you grow up thinking that normal attire for Greek women consisted of black mourning dresses, black scarves, and heavy black shoes with thick heels and black nylons rolled up to just below the knees and tied in a huge knot so that the circulation in their calves and ankles would be severely compromised?

Do you remember your grandmother chasing you around the house with a wooden spoon and, when it broke, screaming, "You broke my spoon, and now I am going to have to kill you!" (Μου εσπασες το κουταλα και τορα πρεπο να σε σκοτωσω!)

Do you remember being sick and having your aunt dressed in a black mourning dress hunched over you and mumbling inaudible Greek phrases as she dropped olive oil into a glass of water and made the sign of the cross on your forehead?

Do you remember your two aunts, suddenly, and for no apparent reason, beginning to spit into the air while they were talking?

Do you remember the time your aunt spat on you three times after she paid you a compliment? And your non-Greek friends, horrified, looking on in disbelief?

Were you ever at home with a non-Greek friend when abruptly your grandmother appeared, chasing your younger brother while screaming, "θα σε σκοτωσω, or θα σε σπασω τα κοκκαλα σου, θα φας ξυλω, or θα σε βρασου!" Do you remember the horrified expression on his face when you casually interpreted this for your friend as, "She's going to kill him, she's going to break his bones, she's going to spank him, or she's going to boil him!"?

Do you remember standing in line to pay at a Greek pizza restaurant when someone in front of you was arguing about the bill and the proprietor muttered in Greek while smiling, "We Greeks were writing philosophy when you were still hanging from trees!" "Ελληνες γραφαμε φιλοσοφια ενω εσεις ακομα κρεμονταν απο τα δεντρα!"

Do you remember walking into the backyard and hearing your father talking to his tomato plants while he was watering them?

Can you remember waking up in the morning and having a tablespoon of castor oil shoved into your mouth and a garlic clove sewn into a small piece of cloth (φυλαχτο) pinned into your pants pocket?

Do you remember your mother chasing you around the house in anger and throwing a slipper at you as you dove under the bed laughing?

Do you remember sitting under a tree in the park on a hot summer day when, suddenly, a car pulled up and five old women dressed in traditional black mourning dresses, with kerchiefs over their heads and carrying sacks, suddenly stumbled out of a car and scampered into the meadow like a group of vultures?

Do you remember that, as soon as you entered the kitchen, regardless of the time of day, your grandmother would insist on you eating a full-course meal, because she determined that you were hungry and needed to gain weight? She obviously never heard of the Mediterranean diet!

These are typical examples—traditions, superstitions, and examples of

INTRODUCTION

homeopathic medicine, to say the least—of what it was like to grow up as a Greek American within a strict Greek community. These are noteworthy traditions that I will never forget, and I am delighted to share them with you. Furthermore, and I think that you will agree, as Greeks, we had, and continue to have, the best of both worlds, Greek and American.

PART I

Being Greek

CHAPTER 1

Greekness

"To be a Greek is not a matter of life but a matter of mind"
—SOPHOCLES

WHERE EAST MEETS WEST, YOU will undoubtedly find a Greek gyro stand and a taverna. The culture of Greece, its topography, and its people's diversity are all reflections of its geographical position between east and west. If you think about it, Greece, in some ways, appears to be the bifurcation between the Western and Eastern worlds, having elements of both. In countries to the west of Greece, the music is different, and instruments such as the guitar are popular. Veal is a popular food, and the land is fertile. In Greece, as in many countries to its east, the climate is arid, lamb is the food of choice, and the music has a Middle Eastern sound; the bouzouki and the clarinet are popular instruments. Its varied topography includes the mountain region, central Greece (Στερεα Ελλαδα), the Peloponnese, and the island groups. Even though each region is a microcosm with its own traditions and cultural identity, Hellenistic traditions common to all Greeks define Greekness.

Many of us have heard the term *Greekness*, but what does it really mean? What does it mean to be a Greek? Does it pertain to physical characteristics, temperament, language, religion, customs, and traditions? According to *The Encyclopedia of Ancient History*,[1] *Greekness*, the state of being Greek, is a term that apparently originated in the second half of the fifth century BCE, when Herodotus stated, "During the Persian wars the Athenians refused to betray the Greeks to the Persians because of their sense of Greekness." Greekness, or *Hellenikon*, in this sense, is a "shared identity based on common blood, language, cult, and way of life." The Hellenic legacy and the concept of Greek pride apparently evolved from the sense of Greekness and imply a strong national identity with language, religion, democracy, personal honor, and responsibility representing core values. These qualities were taught to me informally by my parents and more formally in Greek school when I was young. When I think about common characteristics of this idea of Greekness, at the forefront is our pride in who we are and where we come from.

Pride

In my experience, one of the few things that Greeks agree on is that they feel immense pride in being Greek. Typically, every Greek male thinks he is a descendant of Leonidas or Achilles and feels that the blood of these ancient Greek warriors flows through his veins. Greeks remain adamant that Greece is the cornerstone of Western civilization and continue to draw inspiration from its prolific history. Further, Greeks are quick to remind anyone that democracy, medicine, and the arts originated with us, and we speak with intense pride about Greece being the cradle of civilization and culture. A

---

1 Lynette G. Mitchell, *The Encyclopedia of Ancient History* (New York: Blackwell, 2012), published online 26 Oct. 2012, https://doi.org/10.1002/9781444338386.wbeah09117.

recent study indicated that "Greeks' pride in being Greek surpassed the ethnic satisfaction of every other European nation."[2]

Language

As Greeks, we are in love with our language. (Just ask Mr. Portokalos in *My Big Fat Greek Wedding*, and he will confirm this.) Have you ever driven in a car with a Greek friend or relative when they suddenly notice a bumper sticker on a car with the symbol of a fish and the word ΙΧΘΥΣ? The English translation of ΙΧΘΥΣ is Pisces (fish), and each letter stands for (Ι)ΣΟΥΣ Jesus, (Χ)ΡΙΣΤΟΣ Christ, (Θ)ΕΟΥ God, (Υ)ΙΟΣ Son, and (Σ)ΩΤΗ Savior. They proudly exclaim that those are Greek letters. Further, Greeks are overwhelmed with great pride when a non-Greek makes the slightest attempt to speak Greek, and that person will immediately win the heart of any Greek.

Greek children in my generation were brought up speaking Greek, and English was learned by interacting with non-Greek friends or when we entered primary school. Because most of our social interactions before entering primary school were with Greeks, it remained our primary language until then. You don't have to speak the language to have Greek pride today, because in contemporary society, many Greek Americans who do not speak Greek still have immense pride in their heritage.

National Identity

To complement language, Greekness implies a strong sense of national identity. Uncle Louie, my father's first cousin, told me of an incident that occurred during a citizenship hearing when an official asked my father, "If a war broke out between the United States of America and Greece, who would you fight for?"

---

2 "Greek Culture and Traditions—Where the West Meets the East," Sofia News Agency, April 8, 2010, https://www.novinite.com/articles/115027/Greek+Culture+and+Traditions+-+Where+the+West+Meets+the+East.

My father reportedly replied, "Keep your papers. I would fight for the Greeks!" Finally, when the smoke cleared, the judge awarded my father his citizenship.

I was taught at an early age to stand up as the Greek flag passes by as an example of respect for the Hellenic Republic and its ideals. When I was young, my mother decided that it would be a good idea if I accompanied her to a local theater to see Greek movies with English subtitles. In one of the films, as the Greek military band was marching across the screen, everyone in the audience stood up to abruptly and quickly cross themselves. Initially, I thought the theater must have caught fire, so I started looking for the exits, but I was quickly reminded by my mother that Greeks stand and cross themselves whenever the Greek flag goes by as a sign of national pride and respect. When I contrast this to current events, I can't help but think how times have changed.

Strong Sense of Family

Greekness implies a strong family. Family comes first, and they are always there for you, including extended family and friends as well. In contemporary society, Greeks continue to have a strong sense of loyalty to each other, and they try to help each other whenever they can, regardless of the circumstances.

To cite a personal experience, my uncle Chris, on several occasions, many occurring in the middle of the night and without any prior notice, would place a mattress in his station wagon and drive my father, who was acutely ill, to the hospital ninety miles away. In another example, many years ago, my father drove to Idaho to bring his first cousin, my aunt Mary, and her family back to New Hampshire following the automobile death of her husband. Eventually, when her children grew up and relocated to Southern California, they continuously attempted to convince my father to relocate there.

Maintaining the integrity of the family is critical to Greeks, and it is not uncommon to see relatives working for the same company or families and relatives that own and run the same business. It is a Greek thing to work with someone you can trust—and most often, that means family. Stability, honor, and integrity are characteristics Greeks learn through their family. Wouldn't we be a better society if all children were taught these values at an early age?

Honor

Perhaps the greatest example of Greekness and the highest of the Greek virtues is *filotimo*, the love of honor. Translated, *filo* (φιλω) means friend, and *timo* (τιμω) means honor. Filotimo (φιλοτιμο) represents respect within the Greek family, which is the fundamental template to all facets of Greek life. Greek children are taught personal honor and integrity beginning at an early age. Filotimo represents the sense of right and wrong, respect, and an unconditional love for extended family, elders, friends, and especially for the parents and grandparents who look after them all their lives.

Included within this concept, children and young adults are expected to address all relatives and non-relative elders, as well as adults within the Greek community, as aunt (θεια) or uncle (θειος) out of respect. Respect is so compelling that one's own goals may become abandoned due to concern for displeasing or offending parents or grandparents, an act that remains unforgivable. I have seen young Greeks forgo a college education and enter their father's business, because it was expected of them.

Filotimo (Φιλοτιμο) prohibits airing one's dirty laundry outside the family, requiring that transgressions be kept hidden to avoid exposing or shaming the family, because respect for the family name remains of paramount importance. I was told by my parents, who emphasized the point on several occasions, "Don't embarrass us to ξενι (non-Greeks) or, for that matter, to other Greeks." Honor is a concept we should all embrace. It also implies respect for Greece as a country and for its traditions and customs. Respect, as well as family cohesiveness, is learned at an early age within the Greek home and may represent the foundation by which behavior manifests within the greater society.

Among Greeks, one's word may count more than official papers. Written legal documents were rare in older Greek societies and were replaced by a handshake and the word εγινε, or "It is done!" This is an example of personal honor, and within the Greek community today, in many transactions, this practice remains sufficient to seal the deal. In my experience, Greeks are true to their word and are trusting when others give them their word.

Unfortunately, this rather simplistic tradition has been dishonored in contemporary society, where the spoken word is ignored and even the written word is discounted.

Faith

The intense retention of Greekness can be attributed in large part to our continued devoted affiliation with the Greek Orthodox Church. The church plays a vital role in Greece, perhaps more so than in any other European country, and continues to be especially influential in the United States. Approximately 85 percent of Greeks are Orthodox Christians, and religious practice is integrated into our daily lives as children.

Greeks customarily give a young child a gold cross that has been blessed by a priest. The cross has both traditional and religious significance. When my grandchildren were born, I wanted them to have a cross, and it was important to me that the crosses came from Greece. Therefore, on a trip to Greece shortly after the birth of my twin grandchildren, my primary objective was to find a suitable cross for each of them.

Community

Greeks, in many respects, remain a close society and, in most instances, are more comfortable when with other Greeks. Greeks are compelled to look for other Greeks, no matter how difficult it may be or how far from home we are, and older Greeks continue to retain a distrust of authority, remain more resistant to change, and feel more comfortable within their own Greek neighborhoods.

When I was growing up, the power and importance of the Greek community was undeniable. When I was sick, I went to a Greek physician; my appendix was removed by a Greek surgeon; any dental work I required was performed by a Greek dentist; my hair was cut by a Greek barber; and when I needed clothes, I went to a Greek clothier. Further, our used car was purchased from my uncle Nappy, a car salesman, insured by my uncle Chris, and repaired by my cousin Nick. On rare occasions, generally celebratory in nature—such as a baptism, wedding, or funeral—if we went to a restaurant, it was a Greek restaurant.

Most aspects of my life at that time were Greek, as dictated by my family and by social interactions within our Greek community. This sense of Greekness persists in many Greek communities today. Basically, that's the way it was, and, in many instances, that's the way it is, and that's the way it will be. That's the Greek way. As Gus Portokalos in *My Big Fat Greek Wedding* proclaims, "There are only two types of people: Greeks and those that wished they were Greek!"

Whenever I travel, the first questions that I ask when I reach my destination are, "Where are the Greeks? Is there a taverna nearby? Where is the nearest Greek restaurant?" It may appear inexplicable, but I make it a priority to locate a place where Greeks congregate, because it brings comfort to me to be among Greeks and to hear the language. If you are observant, you will notice that, when Greeks are among Greeks, their eyes brighten, their smiles broaden, and their countenances change. Within minutes, they achieve a greater comfort level and become animated, because they are with family. It's as if they have achieved *kefi* (κεφι), a sense of high spirit and relaxation.

The sense of Greekness that emerges when Greeks congregate includes the presumption that everyone present is Greek. And why not? At a dinner following a recent medical meeting in New York City, an invited representative from the Department of Health in Greece sat to the right of my non-Greek colleague who did not understand Greek. Obviously, assuming he was Greek, she initiated an uninterrupted conversation with him in Greek that continued for more than five minutes, during which time he politely smiled and nodded his head. While this was occurring, I raised my eyebrows, because I knew that he didn't have any idea what she was saying, but I wasn't about to intercede. Nonetheless, she continued her soliloquy, and her "conversation" was interrupted only when the host began his welcoming remarks. An additional impediment to the language barrier in this case is that my colleague is deaf in his right ear. Despite those deficiencies, they appeared to get along, and I don't think she ever realized that he didn't understand anything she was saying!

Hospitality

My parents, and especially my mother, would routinely caution me not to trust a stranger, a non-Greek. Greeks are initially wary of strangers, but these xenophobic characteristics rapidly disappear when strangers show an interest in Greekness. Of course, like anything else, the Greeks also have a word for that, and it is *filoxenia*, a love for foreigners. Initially, because we are a passionate and emotional people, we may tend to misrepresent ourselves to non-Greeks by making ballistic, apparently purposeless arm movements; flashing uncontrollable gestures; and talking noisily. Despite this caricature, we are a warm and friendly people and will always make eye contact when speaking to each other. It is a sign of politeness and directness, as well as a positive cultural aspect.

When we meet you for the first time, we will shake your hand and smile, and if you are a close friend, we will greet you with a hug and a kiss on each cheek and then slap your arm at the shoulder. In my opinion, there is nothing that can compare to Greek hospitality. For those of you who are not Greek, when you visit a Greek home, don't be surprised if you are welcomed as a hospitality gesture with a Greek sweet consisting of sour cherry preserves ("Βισσινο γυκο," "κερασι κουταλιου") in a small crystal glass with a spoon and a tall glass of cold water.

Frugality

My parents, like many Greek families within the Greek section, were very thrifty. Because of our family's limited resources, and partly reinforced by her father's extremely limited income during her childhood within her agora, my mother was especially frugal. My mother never used plastic utensils, paper plates, cups, or napkins, and she would wash plastic bags and plastic margarine dishes with covers and save them so they could be reused. Further, if she packed my lunch in plastic containers and I came home without them, I was reprimanded!

Both my parents used cash exclusively to purchase items and to pay bills. They never had a checkbook or credit cards, and their philosophy was, "If you can't pay for it with cash, then you can't afford it, and therefore, you can't have it!" "You shouldn't spend money that you don't have; it is wasteful."

Incidentally, that principle wasn't unusual for Greeks of my parents' generation. They all operated on a cash-only basis. As a matter of fact, many Greeks, especially those who are first-generation Americans, remain reluctant to utilize credit and retain credit cards. One of the most vivid memories I have of when I was in grammar school is routinely going to the three local sporting goods stores in town looking at, trying on, and holding baseball gloves that we could not afford. Eventually, however, my father surprised me with a new baseball glove just in time for little league tryouts.

My aunt Harriet was the first to purchase a television within our family, and it was a major acquisition. The set was an enormously heavy piece of brown polished oak furniture standing on four stout, stubby legs. In the center of this behemoth of a console was a small, eight-inch circular screen that televised a fuzzy and, at times, unfocused black-and-white picture of individuals who appeared to be in a snowstorm. A large, round, clear plastic channel selection knob inscribed in black with ten channel numbers was situated prominently below the screen and allowed users to select any one of the three available local channels.

On top of the console, an old pair of pliers sat conspicuously on a white embroidered doily. When I asked my aunt why the pliers were there, she replied that the plastic knob with the channel indicators had become worn down due to continued use and no longer fit securely within the metal piece that extended from the console. Therefore, the only way to change the channel was to use the pliers. Of course, I should have known that!

Eventually, the television in the large wooden console exceeded its life span, and the most logical option was to discard it and replace it with a newer model. But that's not the Greek way! Instead, the console was replaced by a much smaller, less cumbersome television that was placed on top of the non-working original console. After all, the former television console was a beautiful piece of furniture, and even if it didn't work, it could not be discarded. I think chances are good that, if I looked hard enough, I could still find that console in some relative's home with the same pair of pliers sitting on a doily.

With the plethora of credit cards, home equity loans, and other lending practices available today, many Americans find themselves in unfortunate financial positions. Perhaps we should pay closer attention to the more sensible fiscal practices of many older ethnic groups, who simply and adamantly stated, "If you can't afford it, you can't have it!" This premise, although disappointing to immediate gratification, is certainly more financially responsible.

Endurance

Greek ethnicity markers and the expression of Greekness were not always advantageous, however. Because of the prevalent winds that blew over this country and the widespread attitude that existed regarding foreigners in the late 1800s and early 1900s, Greek parents and grandparents of my generation vigorously attempted to lose markers of Greekness in an effort to assimilate into American society. They struggled to alienate themselves from terms such as *displaced person*, a term used for someone who immigrated to the United States during that period, primarily from Europe.

Accents identified Greeks as Greeks, and for that reason, last names often were altered to Americanize them and to facilitate assimilation. This attempt at inclusion was similar for other ethnicities as well. As an example, my father's last name was Kosmas, and since there is no *C* in the Greek alphabet, he changed the first letter of his last name from a *K* to a *C*. Although he never provided an explanation for that decision, it was most likely to assimilate. His first cousin Louie, on the other hand, refused to alter his last name from Kosmas to Cosmas, and because of that, some friction remained between them. From this perspective, the argument could be made that my uncle Louie retained a greater sense of Greekness.

I have attempted to understand these Greek characteristics that seem to mark us as Greeks and make us different, but despite our attempts at assimilation, the phrase "It's all Greek to me" persists, and comments such as, "I don't understand anything about these people" carry power and imply that Greeks are different from non-Greeks. If you ask a non-Greek anything about a Greek, more than likely that person will respond by saying, "Don't they own pizza restaurants and operate them with their families, including their children, grandparents, uncles, aunts, and cousins?"

What is the basis of this characterization? Could this concept be propagated by Greeks, and if so, is it a deliberate attempt by Greeks to be different? Or are the Greeks simply victims of a historical calendar? In many respects, admittedly, Greeks differ from most ethnicities in the Western world in regard to language, culture, and traditions. Adding credibility to this concept is the fact that the Orthodox celebration of Easter continues to follow the Julian calendar, while the Western world follows the Gregorian calendar.

This brings us to the next question. Are Greeks simply arrogant, or do they have an inferiority complex? Without a doubt, Greeks are proud and adamant regarding their contributions to the Western world, but in my opinion, they may still have a pervasive feeling of inferiority that developed when they came to America, which they have never overcome.

In an attempt to retain their Greekness, Greeks, like other ethnic groups, tended to form and join organizations and societies that afforded them security. Greek organizations, such as the American Hellenic Educational Progressive Association (AHEPA), the Pan Macedonian Association, the Sons of Pericles, the Daughters of Penelope, and the Pancretan Association of America, provided security and awarded titles to overcome any inferiorities. Conversely, membership in such societies, because of restrictive and exclusionary rules, might be construed as arrogant.

In any event, we were taught by our parents, relatives, and Greek schoolteachers to be proud that we are Greek. Nevertheless, and in spite of this, those of us from immigrant families whose parents were blue-collar workers and worked two jobs may have developed an inferiority complex when we compared our lives to our nonimmigrant counterparts. However, because of the cohesiveness of the Greek family, the close-knit community, and significant contributions from Greek didactic and religious education, as well as Greek society, we endured. And as important, the torch has been passed to my generation to ensure that future generations will achieve and retain a sense of Greekness.

I HOPE I HAVE PROVIDED several useful pieces of information and amusing anecdotes for both my non-Greek readers and Hellenophiles about Greekness that offers a more complete understanding of what it is like to be Greek. Although these fears are not as prevalent in contemporary Greek society, the concern persists, especially among older-generation Greeks, that, as assimilation proceeds, young Greeks will lose important traditions and many cultural aspects of Greek life, as well as their sense of Greekness. And this, of course, gives rise to the conflict that all cultures face. Is it possible to retain Greekness despite assimilation? The retention of Greekness depends on values, traditions, practices, and customs that have been handed down through generations. Greekness cannot be realized and achieved from a textbook. Instead, it must be developed through daily cultural interaction.

And without a doubt, one of the most important characteristics that Greeks share is their belief that the rest of the world envies them for being Greek. Opa!

CHAPTER 2

Passion

"Pathos"

PASSION IS A WORD TAKEN from the Greek word *pathos*, which means "to suffer" (πασχω). Passion is an intense emotion associated with pleasure or pain, which fits the Greeks magnificently. I have seen Greeks arguing vehemently, who will suddenly, in response to the sound of Greek music, get up, clasp hands, and dance enthusiastically, encouraging and praising their previous adversaries' dance steps. And when the dance is over, they all embrace, sit down, drink wine together, and shout "Opa!" This is Greek passion.

We Greeks have a custom of openly portraying our emotions: When Greeks are happy, you know it; when we are sad, it is also obvious; and when we are mad, it's better to be somewhere else. We tend to be animated and loud when talking. And our emotions are magnified by our arms thrashing in what appears to be purposeless ballistic movement patterns that simulate vultures circling their prey.

Greeks Are Headstrong

Greeks love to talk and, regardless of the issue, know everything about anything. Not only do we know everything, but we also do not hesitate to express our opinions about any subject. Therefore, we disagree on everything. Since arguing seems to be a Greek trait, seeing two or more Greeks engaged in a heated discussion is common. In fact, it would not be a typical night at the *kafenion* (coffeehouse) if an argument did not occur.

You can always determine when Greeks are mad when they do not wave with an open hand and the fingers extended; instead, they gesture by suddenly extending their flexed shoulder and extending the fingers from a previously closed fist as if to push the person away. Moreover, the argument may be embellished by saying, "Get lost!" (να χαθεις). I wouldn't blame the casual non-Greek observer for thinking that we might be candidates for neurological examinations. Nevertheless, in most instances, the source argument is eventually forgotten, and the discussion concludes.

Our passion also causes us to be quite emotional. We tend to take everything personally and, as I am often reminded, tend to easily hold grudges. The following incident that occurred in the Greek quarter during the Turkish invasion of Cyprus will verify that. My uncle Tassou settled in Manchester, New Hampshire, with a close Turkish friend who grew up with him in Greece. They would routinely play cards and drink coffee at the local coffeehouse, but despite their close friendship, following the escalation of the Cyprus situation, they became embroiled in a heated argument. Unfortunately, their friendship abruptly disintegrated, and it was never completely restored.

"To Dance Is to Live"

No activity can compare with the Greek dance as an expression of passion, whether of exuberance or melancholy. As film character Alexis Zorba aptly stated, "Dance is an expression of life." Dance has always played an important role in Greek life. Plato said, "The dance, of all the arts, is the one that most influences the soul. Dancing is divine in its nature and is a gift of the gods." And Alexis Zorba exclaimed, "To dance is to live."

When you observe Greeks dancing, you realize that they are celebrating life, that the dancers are alive with passion and, in some instances, dance with some degree of madness. In many respects, the Greek dance is an expression of the dancer's life, expressing such emotions as happiness, sadness, love, and heartbreak. As Alexis Zorba proclaimed when he lost his son Dimitri, "Only the dancing takes away the pain." While everyone else was crying, Alexis Zorba danced. By the final scene in *Zorba the Greek*, when Zorba and Basil danced on the beach in Crete following the collapse of their construction project, we are reminded that passion and hope are inextricably woven. This is a lesson to us that there is a tomorrow and that we should enjoy every day God gives us, despite any setbacks.

One thing is certain—when Greeks dance, they thoroughly enjoy themselves, which is apparent by the expressions on their faces. Whenever we hear music, regardless of our state of mind, the Zorba in us will emerge, because dance is in our blood. On festive occasions, such as Apokries (a holiday when Greeks dress up in costumes; it may be considered analogous to American Halloween and is celebrated in February, before lent), Vasilopita (celebrated on New Year's Day and translated "the sweet bread of Basil"), Sunday afternoon *glendi*, and Church-sponsored dances on weekend nights, the sound of the bouzouki, the clarinet, and the violin become ingrained into our soul.

In ancient Greek society, dances were specific to gender, and men and women were not allowed to dance together. Eventually, if both sexes were included, they were either in separate lines, or the last man and the first woman, usually relatives, were joined not by hand but by a handkerchief, preventing direct contact between the sexes. Further, before a woman could be linked, all the men were included first, and then the women joined. These days, both sexes perform the same dances, and females can also lead. Nonetheless, in some Grecian villages, tradition continues to dictate the order of the dancers' arrangement, generally with the eldest man given the most priority, followed by other men, and then the oldest woman.

The dances, music, and instruments are representative of different regions in Greece and tell unique stories about their ancient warriors and territories. The syrtos, hasapikos, tsamikos, and kalamatianos are considered Panhellenic dances. In addition, many Greeks view the syrtos and kalamatianos as the national dances of Greece.

The syrtos, meaning "dragging dance," is a popular island dance and is characterized by slower, flowing movements (typical of the undulating sea), whereas the kalamatianos has the same basic steps but is bouncy and leaping in character (representative of mountains and varied terrain). The syrtos in the nineteenth century was called Syrtos o Peloponisios and acquired the name kalamatianos from the town of Kalamata in Peloponnesus. It is an open circle dance that moves in a counterclockwise rotation with the dancers holding hands at shoulder height. Holding on to the second person with a handkerchief allows the lead dancer to perform more elaborate steps. The syrtos was referred to in Homer's *Iliad*, and Theokritos described it in the account of Helen's marriage to Menelaus.

The hasapikos, or butcher's dance, apparently originated in Constantinople during the Middle Ages as a battle mime. Having borrowed it from the military, the Greek butcher's guild utilized swords while performing the dance. It is characterized by a lightness of steps and a springiness in the knees and is performed in a straight line with the dancers holding on to each other's shoulders. The syrtaki, also known as Zorba's dance, was created in 1964 for the movie *Zorba the Greek*, and consists of a combination of slow and fast elements of the hasapikos. It begins with slow steps that gradually become more rapid, generally culminating in more adventurous hops and leaps to the haunting sounds of the clarinet and bouzouki.

The tsamikos is the traditional dance of the mountainous regions, and during the Turkish occupation, it was danced by the *armatolos* and *kleftes*, Greek mountain fighters. Because it was an expression of gallantry and bravery, it became designated as the klefthikos and was danced exclusively by men. During holidays or special occasions, it is customarily danced by men in traditional foustanellas—pleated short, skirt-like garments currently worn by Greek Evzones as ceremonial dress. The tsamikos is performed in an open circle to the mesmerizing sounds of the clarinet and bouzouki. It is categorized as one of the "dances of the first," implying a solo for the lead dancer, who will usually hold on to the second person with a handkerchief, providing him with the flexibility to perform various dance moves and leaps, squats, and turns to his skill and self-expression, which is an important part of the Greek dance.

When the tsamikos is danced as a mixed-circle dance, the men traditionally form the outer circle, with the women in the inner circle. Otherwise, the men generally follow the women. This was my father's favorite dance and was representative of the section of Greece where he was from. When he held that handkerchief, you could see the transformation begin that included a change in his facial expression and in his posture. As soon as he heard the music, he smiled in acknowledgment, tilted his head upward as if waiting for instructions from the gods, and then danced. Even when he was very sick, when he heard the clarinet, he struggled to his feet, and he danced. Opa, Charlie (Κοστα)!

In my opinion, the dance that best illustrates Greek passion is the zeibekiko, also known as the "lonely mourning" dance or "dance of the eagle." It is called the lonely mourning dance, because it is performed with intense emotions based on a sense of isolation, despair in life, and pain from within, from an unfulfilled dream. The dancer's steps are improvisational, and the dance is performed with dignity and respect. It is also known as "the dance of the eagle" because when the dancer's arms are open, they symbolize an eagle with its wings spread. The dancer pulls his arms in and bends at the trunk to symbolize supplication to destiny. The word zeibekiko is derived from Zeus, symbolizing the spirit, and from vekos, which means bread, symbolizing the body. The zeibekiko, therefore, symbolizes the divine and the human. It is one of the most popular Greek dances and is representative of the entire spectrum of passion extending from isolation and sorrow to exuberance and happiness. Its origin is traced to Anatolia, today's Turkey, and it was introduced in Greece following the 1922 genocide in Asia Minor with the influx of refugees.

Filled with passion, sadness, and sorrow, the zeibekiko represents the ultimate expression of the Greek soul. While you watch and listen, you can almost share the heartache in the dancer's face as well as the despair in his movements as his arms are spread wide apart and his head is held high, reminiscent of the crucifixion.

"Thou shall not dance zeibekiko if another man has already ordered the song!" According to tradition, there is an order (παραγγελια) to the dance that no one should violate. Since it is a personal dance, it would be humiliating for another man to get up and dance with the man who ordered that specific dance. The zeibekiko is usually performed by one person or by a couple facing each other, with the steps and moves executed in concert to their emotions. Originally performed only by men, women now perform this dance as well, and it is a beautiful dance to watch. No Greek man can watch the zeibekiko without shedding a tear, because it pierces his soul and reminds him that he is a Greek.

We are a passionate and intense people, and the mesmerizing reverberations from the clarinet and bouzouki are likely to catapult us into an altered state of consciousness. This captivating reaction to Greek music has been corroborated by my non-Greek friends as well and is apparent whenever they hear the bouzouki, clarinet, and violin. As soon as the music begins, all conversation abruptly stops, and heads begin to shift from side to side in rhythmic accommodation to the music. Simultaneously, arms are elevated as if they are being lifted by the god's puppeteers, while at the same time fingers extend as if attempting to grasp the heavens. The hypnotic effect of the music thrusts the dancers into an ethereal state, and within minutes, everyone at the table begins to sing and gyrate, screaming *opa* and *yassou* and clapping their hands as commanded by the gods.

PASSION

Recently, I attended a scientific symposium with a non-Greek colleague close to Tarpon Springs, Florida, which is a Greek American sponge diving community. Following dinner at a Greek restaurant, I took him to a Greek nightclub to introduce him to the culture and to provide him with the unique opportunity to experience kefi. Within a few minutes, he became captivated by the sounds of the violin, bouzouki, and clarinet, as well as by the flowing movements of the dancers.

As the night progressed, I noticed that several filled beer bottles began accumulating at our table. Not having requested them, I asked the waiter why they were delivered, and he politely explained that my friend sitting next to me had ordered them. Finally, it became clear to me what had happened. My colleague, obviously having quickly achieved kefi, and while shifting his body in response to the music, maintained his arms extended above his head while repetitively snapping his fingers. Whenever the waiter saw that gesture, he assumed that my colleague was ordering another round of beers. I advised my colleague to keep his arms down or we would never get back to our hotel room. Having achieved kefi, we finally left the nightclub at approximately 3:00 a.m., while the music and dancing continued. We were at dinner recently, and he reiterated that the night at that Greek nightclub was one of the most unforgettable of his life.

Older men and women, Greeks as well as non-Greeks, endure severe pain from debilitating arthritic conditions that affect their mobility and performance of daily activities. Despite their immobility, whenever older Greeks hear the clarinet, the bouzouki, the violin, and the word *opa*, they suddenly become revitalized and ask for a handkerchief. I have seen this scenario repeat itself in many instances. It is as if they are charged by a bolt of lightning hurled by Zeus himself.

When my father was younger, I remember him with great pride as he performed dance moves and leaps effortlessly and skillfully. As he became more arthritic, however, even though his agility deteriorated and the height of his leaps decreased, his determination remained unaffected. Even when he was suffering from an incurable disease later in his life that profoundly affected his mobility, whenever he heard the hypnotic sound of the clarinet, he became mesmerized and drawn in by the Sirens. Although weakened by disease, his spine became more erect, and his eyes would brighten and twinkle as he looked up at the heavens, as if inspired by the gods. And abruptly, as any Greek would in that circumstance, he would ask for a handkerchief, and he danced. Whenever Greeks hear the music, regardless of the reason and of our age or physical condition, even if only for an instant, we all become Zorbas.

Kefi

As most of you are aware, the typical Greek restaurant has little resemblance to its traditional American counterpart. Perhaps the first difference you will notice is that you will be invited to tour the kitchen and to select the fish or meat of your choice. Greeks are proud of their kitchens and the freshness and appearance of their foods, and they are more than willing to open them for inspection. Another difference is the taverna-type atmosphere, modeled after the tavernas scattered throughout Greece. Moreover, many typical Greek restaurants include a small orchestra tucked neatly into a corner that plays Greek music during the evening.

As an additional programmatic attraction, men in authentic Greek outfits may perform dances typical of one or more regions in Greece, and the performance may even include an oriental belly dancer performing sinuous moves intimately close to the diners. And don't be surprised if she selects you to join her in her dance by entangling her scarf around your neck as she pulls you onto the dance floor.

Furthermore, unlike most traditional restaurants that present you with a check shortly after your meal is finished and expect you to leave so the table can be prepared for the next group of diners, you will never be presented with a check at a Greek restaurant until you request it. Traditional Greek hospitality and spirit not only warmly welcome you but encourage you to remain to enjoy the Greek experience, to achieve kefi. Kefi is the attainment of joy, spirit, passion, happiness, the love for life. It does not rely on the intoxicating effects of alcohol and can be attained by listening to exhilarating Greek music. And that includes Greek dancing. And for those who don't know the elements of Greek dance, no worries, the Greeks will gladly teach you the fundamental steps, because we are delighted when someone wants to learn about our culture.

When most restaurants are closing at a reasonable hour to prepare for the next business day, the Greek restaurant, operating on Greek time, opens its eyes and becomes more vibrant, and the search for the attainment of kefi intensifies. Regardless of the hour, any patrons that remain, Greeks as well as non-Greeks, are welcomed to stay, to bond with the restaurant staff, and to continue to enjoy the authentic Greek experience.

This is often when the dancing becomes more animated and continues until the early morning hours. In addition, and familiar to most of us, it is not unusual to see someone suddenly leap from their seat to shower money over the dancers as a gesture of satisfaction with their skill. You may even be invited to throw dishes, breaking them against a wall, as a symbol of good luck. This tradition, however, because of the expense, has been replaced by throwing bouquets of flowers, usually carnations, over the dancers' heads. Take it from me: It is easy to be drawn into an evening of kefi. It is the Greek way.

CHAPTER 3

Chaos

"It's the Greek way"

THAT GREEKS HAVE A PASSIONATE temperament is indisputable, and its expression may resemble chaos. Spontaneity and impulsivity, in many respects, typifies the Greek character. Rather than careful thought before action, Greeks are likely to proceed precipitously at the outset only to pause and reassess before going further. It is kind of a Prometheus/Epimetheus thing. Prometheus thought before he acted, while Epimetheus acted before he thought.

Aunt Mary and Her Chickens

Chaos seems to be the hallmark of my family. Typically, in a Greek family, it is not unusual for someone, particularly an older family member, to have one or more curious idiosyncrasies. Such idiosyncrasies are often associated with aberrant behavior, many times habitual, that may be considered chaotic. This excerpt involving my aunt Mary describes a recurring event from my childhood, and if I hadn't seen it with my own eyes, I never would have believed it. Admittedly, my aunt Mary had several curious idiosyncrasies, but this one was so unusual that I will never forget it.

Under no circumstance would she ever purchase a chicken from a market, because she could never be convinced that it was fresh. Instead, she would have my father drive her to a local chicken farm that had fresh eggs for sale. Imagine the following scenario: The chicken farmer is busily attending to his chickens when suddenly a car rambles up into his long, bumpy, muddy driveway. The noise made by the car rumbling over the driveway creates chaos in his otherwise calm chicken yard. However, things don't settle down after that. Abruptly, the car door opens, and an elderly lady dressed in a traditional black dress, black stockings knotted below the knees, black shoes with thick heels, and a black scarf covering her head stumbles out from the back seat. As she walks, her heels sink into the muddy quagmire. Upon freeing herself, she emphatically notifies the farmer, "You no see, I want a chicken!"

Can you imagine the expression on his face when she assertively confronts him with this mandate? Most likely, he is dumbfounded and doesn't know what she is talking about! She wants to buy a fresh chicken from his chicken yard, and further, she wants to select and catch it herself.

Well, this is precisely what happened when my aunt Mary wanted a chicken. I'm sure the farmer must have thought she was eccentric at best, and her request was outrageous. He was rendered dumbfounded and speechless, at least for a moment, after which he would turn to me and ask, "Is she kidding?"

I would reply, "No, absolutely not!"

I can't imagine what she said in her heavy Greek accent or how she convinced him, and I'm not sure she did, but he was probably so incredulous that he didn't know how to react to her demand. But she got her chicken and advised him that she would be back. He must have trembled whenever she returned, and she did so periodically. Regardless of the season or the weather, whenever she needed a fresh chicken, this remarkable spectacle would repeat, every time with her dressed in her traditional black mourning dress with black stockings knotted just below the knees, complete with heavy black shoes and thick heels.

There she stood, in the muddy chicken yard with her arms on her hips in a battle-ready position, both eyes focused, surveying the battlefield, looking for the most suitable prey, reminiscent of Patton as he examined his battlements. Once locked onto her target, she would lurch forward and trudge through the soggy farmyard, determined to capture her prey.

At the same time, the frantic chicken, aware that it had been targeted, and seeing the black-draped enemy charging toward it, would immediately take flight. Flapping its wings, with its neck fully extended, clucking noisily, and making sharp, angular turns, the chicken would attempt to escape from the black-cloaked demon who was chasing it. Chickens are almost impossible to catch.

The chase would continue, and regardless of how long it took, Aunt Mary eventually fatigued her prey, captured it, and turned it over to the farmer, who agreed to prepare it for her. The term *free-range chicken*, currently in vogue, apparently is not a new phenomenon in poultry farming after all. We had "free-range chickens" in those days; just ask my aunt Mary!

This is one of the inconceivable events that will remain imprinted in my mind for the rest of my life, and I can visualize it as if it happened yesterday. The sight of my aunt Mary trudging perilously through the chicken yard, attempting to catch a cackling, wing-flapping chicken was preposterous. An inconceivable adventure? Yes! Difficult to believe? Absolutely not! Not if you are a Greek of my generation and have an eccentric family member like my aunt Mary. When she moved to San Diego, California, her daughter had to find another chicken farm, and the cycle began again!

Uncle George Takes to the Sky

My uncle George, one of Aunt Mary's sons who lived in San Diego, California, recently came back to Manchester, New Hampshire to visit his old navy buddies. Despite being active and feisty, because he was eighty-eight years old, his family thought it would be a good idea if he flew with his sister, Evangeline, who was eighty-four. While in Manchester, he complained of dizziness and shortness of breath, and despite his obstinacy, he was admitted into the Veterans Administration hospital for observation. The doctors determined that he had suffered a cardiac event that required hospitalization and further testing.

Despite the preliminary diagnosis, this was not in my uncle's plan, and he was not going to have anything to do with it. My aunt and I pleaded with him to remain hospitalized until the testing could be completed, and we advised him that his departure would be against medical advice. I wasn't surprised that our efforts fell on deaf ears, and within the next few minutes, chaos ensued in his hospital room. My uncle George put his clothes on and abruptly walked out of the hospital while we and the hospital staff stood in disbelief.

My horrified aunt Vangy and my uncle George checked into a hotel and flew back to California the next morning. Fortunately, he remained asymptomatic and healthy for several years following that incident. This is just another example of Greek chaos.

Incidentally, my uncle George died last year at age ninety-five, and my cousin Addison, who is a pilot, spread his ashes over Lake Coeur d'Alene, Idaho, where Uncle George had lived as a young boy before my father brought him and his family to Manchester. My uncle George returned home!

BEING A GREEK, YOU REALIZE that chaos can develop in an instant and can manifest itself in several ways. *Chaotic* is a good word to describe most Greeks, especially those of us who seem to lack the patience for attending to meticulous detail in solving any problem. When we fall into this category, and I confess that I do, then our attitude is, "If this is the problem, then obviously, that must be the solution." It remains incredible, but you can rest assured that if Greeks don't know the answer to a question, they will make something up, quickly and rather convincingly. And if that doesn't work, or if it is not the right answer, then it is *your* fault.

Greeks will tell you what they are thinking as soon as the thought enters their mind, and they prefer to solve conflicts right away rather than let any disagreement go, even if the solution is erroneous. If you want to get into an animated discussion with a Greek, simply express your opinion about any subject and wait for the chaos to begin, because every Greek has a correct opinion regarding any issue. By simply expressing your opinion about an issue, before you know it, you will be confronted by animated Greeks flailing their arms, outshouting one another, each with a different but correct opinion. An old Greek proverb that many Greeks seem to follow at the Hartford Hellenic Cultural Center is, "It is easier to talk than to hold one's tongue!"

The Hellenic Cultural Center Gets a New TV

The Hellenic Cultural Center, in addition to serving as a refuge for Greeks, is the site of many amusing incidents that exemplify the Greek temperament and the Greek opinionated personality. The Center had recently purchased a new, large flat-screen television that would provide greater clarity for community members to watch soccer games, Greek soap operas, and news from Greece. It arrived with a wall bracket and detailed directions for fastening the television securely to the wall.

A construction crew was hastily assembled that included four Greeks equipped with tool belts and the self-proclaimed necessary proficiency to securely attach the television to the wall. At least, that's what we thought. The project was ready to begin, but unfortunately each member had his own correct opinion regarding the installation, and you can imagine what followed. The project no sooner began than it rapidly deteriorated into absolute chaos.

Following an exhaustive and fiery discussion regarding the suitability of a wall installation (and I still believe it was because they lacked the collective knowledge necessary for a secure placement), the crew ultimately determined that the television should be temporarily placed on an old warped, wobbly wooden stand approximately four feet high and set up the TV as if it were a god on a pedestal. When I looked at that stand, I was incredulous, and to say that it was unsteady was a gross underestimation.

Nevertheless, the decision was made, the stand put into position, and the television placed on it. The crew skillfully secured it, and the project received the Greek construction seal of successful completion and approval.

The next night, when I went to the Hellenic Cultural Center, the television and the stand were missing. However, they had hired an independent mechanic, who was securing a bracket to the wall in preparation for another new television. I don't think I need to tell you that the wobbly stand collapsed and sent the television to Hades.

Greek Time

An amusing yet intriguing illustration of the chaotic characteristic of Greeks is the Greek concept of time. Greek time is totally different from real time. The Greeks are notorious for ignoring punctuality and customarily arrive late to most social events, and I maintain that they purposely attempt to defy time whenever they can. They have designed their own set of rules with criteria that seem to be standard and perfectly acceptable.

Arriving at least a half hour late for an event is considered punctual and, in certain instances, may be early. If Greeks are invited to a party at someone's home, they will likely drive by in a car, look into a window to see how many people have arrived, and if they think too few people are present, will circle the block a few more times before even thinking of arriving. I have been in a car with Greeks when this occurred. And by no means is this idiosyncrasy an isolated circumstance or limited only to informal events; I've seen it happen during formal events as well.

An example of Greek time and the ensuing chaos occurred when I attended a Greek scientific symposium in Montreal, Canada, recently. I was reminded by telephone on Friday evening by the event chairperson that my lecture was scheduled for 8:00 a.m. on Saturday morning. I arrived at the hall ten minutes before my lecture to prepare my slide presentation and was astonished to find that the auditorium was empty. Typically, by this time, at least a few people would be present, but not at this symposium. Remarkably, when no one had arrived by 8:00 a.m., I began to think I had the wrong day and time. Did I imagine that I had received that phone call the previous evening? I began to doubt my sanity at this point. Bewildered, I left the lecture hall and walked into the large adjoining foyer only to see clusters of people eating bagels, drinking coffee, and conversing.

Having spoken at previous scientific and medical symposia, punctuality was a priority. But not this time. Not with the Greeks! I was aware of Greek time, but I didn't think it extended to formal events such as this one. Nonetheless, I laughed quietly, poured myself a coffee, and waited patiently for evidence that the session was about to begin. Approximately a half hour later, without any explanation, the participants began to casually saunter into the lecture hall, and after the greeting and opening remarks by the chairperson, the moderator introduced me as the first speaker, and the session began.

CHAOS! IMPULSIVITY! AN ACT FOLLOWING an impulsive thought. Often with catastrophic effects, unless there is a pause followed by more rational behavior. Is it exclusively a Greek phenomenon? Of course not. Do some Greeks exhibit this characteristic? Of course they do, as do some people of all cultures. This is another example that we are all more alike than we are different.

PART II

The Greek Community

CHAPTER 4
The Agora

"Remain within me, and I shall protect you, always!"

GREEK MIGRATION BEGAN IN THE 1700s and, like other cultures, was catalyzed as a method for Greeks to escape hardship and to begin to build a better life for themselves and their families. Generally, Greeks, like other ethnic groups, came to the United States with little formal education and no money, and through hard work, they established viable Greek American communities, the *agoras* (Χωρι), that have flourished through generations and have provided for the protection and the perpetuation of the Greek identity in the United States.

Approximately three million residents in the United States are of Greek ancestry. Many Greek immigrants stayed in the East as laborers, shoe shiners, and dishwashers in major metropolitan areas, while others headed west to work on the railroads or in mines in the Midwest and West. However, because of competition with other ethnic cultures and immigrants from other countries, Greeks had to look for alternative economic opportunities, and many ended up in the restaurant business or other service industries.

Current estimates have approximately one hundred thousand Greek

Americans living in the Boston-Worcester-Manchester and New Hampshire areas. Mainly due to industrial opportunities, large numbers of Greek immigrants settled in communities along the Merrimack River in New England and found employment in shoe factories and textile mills. From here, the Greek communities, the agoras, developed and allowed for the maintenance and perpetuation of Greek traditions, customs, and life.

My Father Comes to America

Where does my story as a Greek American start? Perhaps an appropriate beginning would be when my father left his mountainous village of Anthousa (known as Lepinitsa before 1928) in the municipal unit of Aspropotamos in Trikala, in the Pindus mountains of Northern Greece. He left as a teenager, seeking a better life, and came to America by ship.

As many immigrants did, he documented his age as being older than it actually was to secure passage and to gain entrance into the United States of America. It must have been extremely difficult for my father and his family when they made the ultimate decision that he would immigrate to America. He was only sixteen years old, and the realization that he was going to leave his family must have been extremely painful, especially since he and his family knew they were not likely to ever see each other again. Nonetheless, as distressing as it must have been, they made the sacrifice, recognizing that his potential for a better life was in America.

My father never spoke about that period in his life. What an unimaginably courageous decision that had to have been for those families, no matter the country, who knew they would never see their children again, and also for the children and young men and women as they made the horrific voyage in crowded, unsanitary ship steerage compartments and finally arrived in the United States, most not speaking English, and attempted to establish a new life. My father eventually settled in Manchester, New Hampshire.

Like other immigrants, once he arrived, he was required to fill out citizenship applications, insurance forms, and legal documents, and as you can imagine, because he had falsified his age initially, he forgot the date he had recorded, which eventually created difficulties for him and our family. When circumstances developed that required documentation of his age, inconsistencies were found. Nevertheless, I don't remember it becoming a serious issue until after his death, when chaos erupted as my mother attempted to collect life insurance benefits. Because the age on his policy was different when compared to his other documents, the process was awkward, but it was eventually resolved. In defense of my father, changing one's age was common for those seeking to immigrate to America during that period. My father talked about his family and described his village to me on several occasions, but he never did return to Greece and sadly never again saw his family there.

My Agora

Manchester, New Hampshire, typical of many industrial cities along the Merrimack River, was home to shoe factories and textile mills and was comprised of different ethnicities, principal among them Greek, Irish, Polish, French, and German. Even though they were clustered within the center of the city, primarily due to economic constraints, they tended to establish distinct ethnic neighborhoods. With undaunting regularity, and fueled by an intense work ethic, Manchester's multiethnic immigrant workers would leave the sanctuary of their respective "sections" early every morning and pour into the mill yards and the shoe factories situated along the banks of the Merrimack River. For the most part, and for most of the immigrants, any interaction with other ethnicities occurred at work, and that was the extent of assimilation.

At the end of a long workday, workers would return to their homes, where the women would assume the responsibility for the children and the men would congregate at a men's social club. With the Greeks, that club was the kafenion within the agora. This lifestyle ensured the retention of important ethnic and cultural values. This country was built by immigrants, and the various ethnic sections contributed to its strength by maintaining ethnic values and cultural traditions. Elimination of these ethnic sections, in my opinion, weakens the framework of our country.

To us, the agora was an ethnic sanctuary, and we were comfortable and secure within its boundaries. Other ethnicities worked within it and shopped in it, but when the day ended, once again it became exclusively a Greek place.

I hope, by providing a detailed and rather graphic description of the agora as it appeared when I was growing up, to illustrate the conditions in which many Greeks and other ethnic cultures lived in the United States. The newer generation of Greeks might also understand what life was like for their parents and what their parents encountered as they worked to make life better for their children and succeeding generations.

My father was an advertising manager for a regional Greek newspaper, and that required traveling to various cities in northern New England to secure advertisements. While traveling with him, I quickly began to realize that the agora I was brought up in was not a unique ethnic community but was quite typical of other agoras in the Merrimack Valley.

The agora, or the Greek section, as it was called in Manchester, New Hampshire, consisted of an unsightly collection of rundown, weathered, dreary, and generally poorly maintained three-story crumbling wooden commercial buildings and dull-gray, worn residential tenements that resembled a shantytown located inside the city limits. It was situated in the southern section of the city and occupied approximately a five-square-block area surrounded to the north by the Polish section and to the east by the Irish section.

Bordering the Greek section to the west were the woolen mills and shoe factories aligned along the east side of the Merrimack River. Directly across the river on the west side were large French and German sections. The French comprised the largest immigrant population, and in addition to occupying a section next to the Germans on the west side, they established a second community on the eastern border of the city. None of the ethnic sections would have won a prize for architectural beauty.

Due to austere economic limitations, most Greeks lived within walking distance of the mills, shoe factories, markets, and shops and were within one-half mile of the city's center, making automobile ownership, which was economically not feasible for most families, fortunately unnecessary. Most of the Greeks lived on the third floor of rickety tenements, because they featured the least expensive rents. In addition to their gloomy and unattractive appearance, the buildings were neglected and never renovated. Recently, in the name of progress, the Greek section was largely eradicated and replaced by a civic center with an auditorium and an indoor skating rink. Bluntly stated, in the name of progress, an ethnic community was eliminated.

In the center of the Greek section, and comprising its heart, was a disgustingly unattractive, barren, dirt-filled rectangular park that encompassed one block, named after General George Kalivas, a Greek war hero. It was bordered by Pine Street to the east, Lake Avenue to the north, Spruce Street to the south, and Chestnut Street to the west. In the park's center, General Kalivas's former bronze and currently tarnished, weathered green statue stared down in disappointment over a nonfunctional disintegrating stone water fountain filled with tin cans, broken glass bottles, and other debris.

Unlike many typical well-manicured parks in other parts of the city, the conspicuously absent grass had been replaced by dirt scattered with broken glass fragments and trash. The few light posts that remained intact were placed at regular intervals along either side of a crumbling tar path that coursed through the park, but most fixtures had broken glass and were inoperative, providing for a dreary area and an unfriendly atmosphere in the evening. Lining the path were crumbling cement benches with wooden slats that were either absent or splintered, prohibiting anyone from sitting. The geographical demarcations of the park were defined by a one-foot-high decaying cement wall that separated it from four busy streets in the heart of the agora. The inadequately maintained park fit in most appropriately with its dreary surroundings.

Scattered throughout the Greek section were four coffeehouses: one on Pine Street, one on Chestnut Street, and two on Spruce Street that were characterized by a dirty film on their large front windows and dim interior lighting that prohibited anyone from seeing inside with any clarity. However, if you looked more closely, you were able to distinguish the silhouettes of seated men hunched over, either playing cards, reading newspapers, or simply appearing to be staring aimlessly while twirling their *komboloi*, Greek worry beads, with a cup of demitasse coffee on a table in front of them.

Within this aggregate of substandard buildings on Pine Street, on the east side of Kalivas Park, was the Hellenic Community Center, referred to by the students as the Greek school, a typical old rectangular, three-story wooden building with a white wooden facade at its entrance, on top of which stood a gold painted cross. The Center was sandwiched between other three-story, dilapidated wooden tenement buildings, one with a coffeehouse on the first floor and apartments above.

It remains fascinating how the mind captures and retains specific events and images, regardless of how insignificant they appear to be at the time. I remember throwing a snowball at one of my friends before Greek school one winter afternoon. I missed and broke the coffeehouse window, bringing the card game inside to an abrupt halt. Following a rapid apology to an understanding coffeehouse manager, the situation was resolved by a promise to repair the broken pane. In the meantime, to retain the heat, one of the men placed an old Greek newspaper over the open pane, secured it with tape, and the card game continued.

Unlike the cheerfulness of the American school building characterized by wide, airy corridors and bright classrooms decorated with posters and brightly colored walls, the Hellenic Community Center displayed its unique personality, and I imagine you could call it a sense of Greekness. Whenever we entered the bleak foyer of the Hellenic Community Center, we were immediately confronted by a collection of dusty and weathered, gold, wood-framed photographs of past priests, as well as frowning church council members, suspended on a dark gray wall. Characterized by their handlebar moustaches and thick, bushy eyebrows, their scowling expressions and glaring eyes reinforced the bleakness of the entrance and prompted us to walk by tentatively and unobtrusively. Their countenances seemed to be reminding us why we were there.

Beyond the foyer on the first floor was the priest's office on the left, followed by a small meeting room and restrooms. Two small meeting rooms and a kitchen occupied the right side and were used for Junior GOYA (Greek Orthodox Youth of America) meetings, small youth dances, and church council meetings, the latter of which had to be intriguing, because trying to get a group of Greeks to agree on anything is virtually impossible.

Extending on either side of the dreary, uninviting entry foyer were stairs leading to the upper floors. The second floor housed the Greek school, where daily classes provided formal educational instruction in Greek, which included language, history, culture, conversational skills, reading, writing, respect, and discipline.

The third floor opened into a large hall with an elevated stage at the far end secured by Greek and American flags on either side. The hall was primarily used for celebratory events, such as Greek Independence Day, but after a GOYA basketball team was organized, it could be hastily converted into a makeshift basketball court complete with basketball goals. Unfortunately, it lacked a locker room and showers, and except for special events, the heat was always turned off, making the first few minutes of practice unpleasant. Nonetheless, we were ecstatic to have a place to play basketball, and it eventually became the home court of the Manchester GOYA basketball team. The elevated stage at the end of the hall, however, provided an amphitheater for us to demonstrate (to our horror) our oratory skills on Greek Independence Day and other Greek holidays.

Diagonally to the left of the Greek Community Center, on the southwest side of Kalivas Park, on the corner of Spruce and Chestnut Streets, opposite the Pine Grove Cemetery, and situated on a tenement building's first floor, was a variety store with a conspicuous large red sign with white letters that read *ART NOVELTY*. It was a variety store, Greek style, and it sold candy, Greek newspapers, favors, and magic tricks. Whenever we had any money, we would buy penny candy there before Greek school classes. I remember it vividly, with several small Greek flags hanging from twine and displayed prominently in the large front windows.

Several large, colorful posters depicting various Greek sites covered the interior walls. Without question, this was a Greek place. Because the large, front, flag-covered window blocked the sunlight, the interior was dusky, and I remember that the old uneven, weathered, wooden floor creaked as we walked around. A large tarnished, silver-colored cash register was perched on the front counter, where it was prepared to swallow our nickels in exchange for candy. In contrast to the *ART NOVELTY*, diagonally across the street and on the opposite corner was a brightly painted, well-lit Greek market that sold produce, fruit, and meat—nothing of any interest to us kids.

Lake Avenue provided the northern border of Kalivas Park and extended to Elm Street, representing the commercial heart of the Greek section. It was comprised of a series of dilapidated wooden structures on either side that were business related on the first floor and residential above. Approximately halfway down and on the left side of Lake Avenue on the first floor of a badly maintained wooden building was the Van Otis chocolate shop. Despite its exterior facade, its interior was immaculate, and its workers created chocolate of the highest quality. The owner was a relative of ours, and my mother worked there in the evenings. I remember that she would come home with several chocolates and was proud that she could identify the filling by the design on the exterior of the chocolate. Since the Greek section has now been decimated, Van Otis has relocated to another location within the city. It continues to operate and remains recognized for the excellent quality of its chocolates.

Across the street and opposite to Van Otis Chocolates, on the first floor of an equally run-down tenement building, was the *Acropolis* Greek-English newspaper office, identifiable only by the faded blue lettering with black trim painted on the smudged large front window. The cluttered interior was so

THE AGORA

dark, shadowy, and disheveled that I couldn't understand how any productive work could be accomplished or, moreover, how a newspaper could be printed in that chaos.

Although there were several *kafenia*, or coffeehouses, in the Greek section, the one that my father preferred was approximately half a block down from Kalivas Park on Lake Avenue. It occupied the first floor of a shanty-like three-story gray wooden building and was wedged in between the *Acropolis* Greek-English newspaper office and a cobbler shop. The kafenion was an integral part of my father's life, as it was with most Greek men of that generation. He would play cards there while I was at Greek school, and he would frequently go there in the evenings when he wasn't working, because it was a Greek thing to do. Since it was close to the Hellenic Community Center, I would walk there to meet him when Greek school finished.

The coffeehouse was identifiable by the words *ΕΛΛΕΝΙΚΟΝ ΚΑΦΕΝΙΟΝ* (Greek Coffeehouse) visible in bleached white letters with faded blue trim on a large front window clouded by a dirty coating due, at least in part, to persistent cigarette and cigar smoke, as well as to inattention. I remember peering through that opaque window routinely to see whether my father was there.

St. George Greek Orthodox Church, the largest of the Orthodox churches in the city, was originally located on Pine Street on the southernmost point of the Greek section. Since that time, however, it has been relocated and expanded and has been designated a cathedral. Since many social activities were organized by the Church, it represented a powerful influence in Greek life.

For the most part, the agora was where I grew up. It was our world, and we weren't much aware of what was happening outside it. Except for attending American school in the daytime, the agora was where we could be found. We lived and played there. We were most comfortable there because that is where the Greeks were. But please understand that this was not a deliberate attempt by the Greeks to segregate themselves from other ethnic groups. Instead, it evolved as a result of ethnic cohesivity, a commonality of language, traditions, religion, and culture. This was typical of other ethnic communities within the city as well. They all had their agoras. This may be described as cultural isolation to some degree and a failure of assimilation in the strictest sense. Nonetheless, it ensured that ethnic and cultural values remained integral.

Many aspects of Greekness—exemplified by emphasis on the closed, more dependable agora reminiscent of an isolated mountain village—appear to be dissolving today. However, older Greeks continue to retain a historical distrust of authority, remain more resistant to change, and feel more comfortable within identifiable ethnic neighborhoods complete with their agoras, churches, and coffeehouses that allow them to more easily retain their cultural and ethnic values.

CHAPTER 5

Family

"Are all these people in your family?"

THE GREEK FAMILY! OH, THE Greek family! How do you define it? Conjugate members, grandparents, relatives, and friends. And as my non-Greek friends would ask, "Are all these people in your family?"

"Yes, all these people are in my family!" That's the way it is. As Greeks, everything revolves around the family. It continues to be the fundamental unit of support and identity, both emotionally and financially, and like many other ethnic groups, we strive to ensure that our values will be handed down to succeeding generations.

Traditionally, Greek families tend to be extremely close, and strong bonds are formed and maintained, not only between all members of the conjugal family but among extended family members and friends as well. As a matter of fact, to most Greeks, all Greeks are considered family. And perhaps that should be a lesson to all of us, that despite our differences, we are all part of an extended family.

The Greek Family

The father, in most Greek families, is the outside representative and enjoys social respect, but the mother is the organizer of the house, the mediator in family disputes, and the preserver of family unity. Admittedly, even though the Greek woman is the domineering person within the household in most circumstances, until only recently, she remained at home and in a submissive position to her husband; likewise, her opinions and attitudes regarding financial and external affairs remained relatively unimportant. However, as Maria Portokalos in *My Big Fat Greek Wedding* appropriately stated, "The man is the head, but the woman is the neck, and she can turn the head any way she wants." Fortunately, gender differentiation has declined dramatically in contemporary Greek society, and the elevation of the woman's position within the family was enhanced by the abolition of the dowry as recently as 1983.

Children are very special in Greek society, and they are showered with love and attention by parents, grandparents, and relatives. Furthermore, as far as Greeks are concerned, hugging appears to be synonymous with suffocation. My grandchildren still laugh when they remember how firmly they were hugged by their great-grandmother. They must have said to each other as she approached, "Oh no, here comes yia yia! Take a deep breath, and try to relax!" Those asphyxiating embraces Greek children endured made them feel as if their ribs were going to crack and their chests would collapse.

In addition to hugging, grandparents, uncles, aunts, and even older cousins would stroke my head and pinch my cheeks until they became tender and inflamed. And to make matters worse, concerned that I might have a fever because of my red cheeks, my mother or one of my aunts would take my temperature (and not by the oral route). I think of those times and laugh whenever I stroke my grandchildrens' heads and hug them, which I do whenever I see them. I can't help myself. This display of affection has been passed down to me through the generations. Without question, children are especially important in a Greek family, and they know that they are loved.

The term *extended family* has no meaning for the Greeks, because they consider grandparents and relatives to be nuclear family members as well. The scarcity of retirement homes in Greece confirms the importance of the extended family, and within the Greek family, it is still common to see three generations living together. Multigenerational living remains customary, because Greeks have a great respect for age and revere their older relatives.

Many Greek families with living grandparents live this way, because it provides a purpose and security for the elders, as well as guidance and wisdom to the children, ensuring that filotimo (respect) will be preserved. In addition, another Greek custom is to maintain a strong relationship with our married children and, if possible, for them to remain close to us, because it increases the likelihood that traditional values will be maintained and strengthened. In many instances, children will strive to choose the same occupation/profession as their father, especially if the family's social and financial situation is secure.

My friends from Rhodes own a restaurant and operate it as a family business with their sons, their wives, and extended family members. My wife and I live for our children and grandchildren, and we are happiest when they are with us. Moreover, we are most fortunate that our daughter and her family live close to us, enabling us to have daily interaction with them, notwithstanding that we provide them with easily accessible and reasonable babysitting services.

My conjugal family included my mother, father, and me. Despite a strong attachment between us, relations were rather formal and seemed to remain that way for the most part, at least until I became older. When I was younger, I don't remember either parent telling me they were proud of me, but that didn't appear to be unusual for children in Greek families of that generation. Basically, that was the way things were in those days.

When I think about it, respect for parents and all family members, as well as proper behavior in all circumstances, was expected, so why should a parent tell you they were proud of you for doing what was expected? In contrast, even though Greek parents did not tell their children directly how proud they were of them, they would sing a thousand songs (or χίλια τραγούδια) about them to other family members and friends in their absence. Strange, those Greeks. Perhaps, partly because of my experiences, I feel strongly that it's important to constantly remind our children how proud we are of them, and I hug my grandchildren without trying to suffocate them whenever I have the opportunity.

Greek Mothers

"Enyo" (Ενυω), the "Greek goddess of war," could describe Greek mothers. The best description of a Greek mother came from my good friend Chris, who once emphatically remarked that "all of our mothers were tough, but Artie's mother? Boy, she was something else!" A Greek mother is controlling, restrictive, and overprotective to the point where it is smothering and refuses to admit that her children have grown up. Moreover, she is never wrong, regardless of the issue, and will continue to emphasize that "no one will love you like I do!" There is another characteristic that Greek mothers have—they will protect their children under any circumstance and at all costs.

My mother, like many Greek women, had a robust figure and, like me, blue eyes, the latter characteristic shared by only 25 percent of Greeks. Typical of many young Greek women of that generation, her formal education ended with the completion of high school. Nonetheless, Greek families of that generation expected that a young woman, following the completion of high school, should marry a Greek man and start a family, and that's what my mother did. My mother remained at home until I was old enough to attend school, and then she worked in a shoe factory located a mile from our home.

My mother worked along with many other Greek American women, as well as women of other ethnicities, and despite difficult work conditions, they developed a comradery that seemed to convert work into an acceptable social environment. I remember she had many friends, and it was a very cheerful time for her. As I recall that time, it may have been the most contented period in her life. She would walk to work in the morning and return at noon to provide lunch for me, since the school did not have a cafeteria, and then she'd walk back to work for the afternoon.

Eventually, when the shoe factories closed, and primarily because of her restless character, she became a teacher's assistant for young special needs students. Despite the gratification she achieved from that experience with the students (she was designated teacher's assistant of the year), during that time, and perhaps partly because of the closure of the shoe factories, her social interactions with her friends decreased, and she began to withdraw back into her family.

As in most Greek families, my mother was the principal figure within the family, partly because my father worked late hours and had two jobs. There was no mistake about it. She was the dominant person, certainly not only to be respected but to be feared as well. To say that my mother was volatile would be an understatement.

Typical of many Greek women, my mother appeared to suffer from an undefined, restless type of anxiety that appeared to develop and become more progressively obvious as she became older and had to stop working. When she was younger, during the years when I was in grammar school, she seemed to be able to control her restlessness by always being on the go, frequently visiting her sisters or friends after work, or by watching softball games at Wolfe Park in the evenings. (This latter activity most likely evolved from her love for baseball and from her reported success as a softball pitcher in high school.)

To ease this restless feeling, we would travel to Boston to visit godchildren or my mother's sister, Victoria, or travel by automobile to West Virginia to visit relatives. On one momentous occasion, we drove to Hempstead, New York, to a Greek church to see an icon of the weeping Virgin Mary. I remember standing in line outside the church in the blistering summer heat for what seemed like an eternity, waiting for a chance to see the icon.

Perhaps the most revealing example of her restlessness was the trip that she and I took to San Diego, California, during the summer when I was fifteen years old, to visit our relatives who had been attempting to coerce us to relocate there. Because her anxiety prohibited her from flying, she arranged for us to travel nonstop by bus from Manchester, New Hampshire. Despite several attempts, I failed to convince her that this was madness. And so, it began. Departing from the Manchester, New Hampshire bus station in the early morning, it became a three-and-one-half day continuous nightmare that included sleeping on the bus and that finally ended mercifully mid-morning in San Diego. The two weeks in Southern California were great, but continuously lurking in the back of my mind was the impending return trip home, which, by the way, turned out to be equally horrendous.

Typical of many Greek women, my mother was strong willed and attempted to retain her independence well into her nineties. Perhaps the most appropriate example of her unrelenting vitality and self-sufficiency was holding on to her freedom by maintaining her driver's license so she could continue to drive. Concerned that her motor skills might be deteriorating, I attempted to convince her on several occasions that perhaps she should consider not driving and graciously donate her car to charity. That request, of course, in addition to being insulting, fell on deaf ears.

Incidentally, her hearing was becoming increasingly impaired, and following numerous appeals for her to get a hearing aid, and as she exclaimed, "Only to satisfy you," much to her chagrin, she relented, and I was able to get her fitted. As expected, she never admitted that her hearing had improved. To inform me of how thoughtless and insensitive my recommendations regarding her ability to drive were, on one visit when she was ninety-five years old, she apprised me smugly that she had recently passed a driver's test and proceeded to show me the validation. It was hard to believe, but she had the documentation. The instructor at the test site must have asked her to turn on the ignition and quickly decided that his life was worth more than the nightmare that was about to unfold before him. My guess is that he congratulated her, gave her the license, and jumped out of the car as quickly as he could.

Later, whenever I would examine her car, I would notice the ever-increasing presence of longer scratches and deeper, more extensive dents and gouges. Following a snowstorm, she telephoned and advised me that the car—not her, mind you, but the car—had inadvertently driven through an intersection and somehow collided with a snowplow. After determining that she wasn't injured, apprehensively, I asked her what happened next, and she replied, "Well, I got out and informed the driver that I was a senior citizen and that if he did not report it to my insurance, I would give him one hundred dollars!" He replied, "Lady, there's no damage to my plow, but look at your front end!" No money was exchanged in that incident, and they both drove away. I can only imagine what the man driving the snowplow must have been thinking.

Despite her protests, my mother's motor functions continued to deteriorate, and her ability to drive the car continued to diminish precipitously, while her ability to aim it improved markedly. Ultimately, her car began to look like an accordion on wheels. I continued to try to persuade her to give the car to charity, but she defiantly clung to her last vestige of independence despite my efforts to convince her that giving up driving was for her safety as well as that of others.

In desperation, one afternoon, without her realizing it, I went out to the driveway and removed several vital organs from the car's engine compartment. The next evening, she called me and explained that the car had failed to start that morning, but she had called the local Greek mechanic, who came and put in $400 worth of parts. Of course, the car started immediately, and she happily drove away. Remarkable? Not really! In retrospect, I should have called him and alerted him regarding my intention. Eventually, when she was in her late nineties, after extensive pleading, I finally convinced her to donate the car to charity. The driving test that we had hoped my mother would fail finally occurred while she was a resident at the nursing home when she was denied the use of a motorized wheelchair because of repeated damage to the walls, as well as to other patients' shins.

During one visit to her apartment when she was in her midnineties, she revealed that she had a small amount of cash safely concealed in a small locked metal box on the floor of a metal closet in her bedroom. Further, she disclosed that the key to the metal box was securely hidden behind a small tomato plant that sat on the windowsill adjacent to her bed. She wanted me to know this in the event of an emergency. When I went into her bedroom to check, I was astonished to find that the key was on the windowsill next to the tomato plant as she had described, but it was totally exposed and clearly visible in the afternoon sunlight. More astonishing, the metal closet door was open, and the metal box on the floor was completely exposed, unlocked, and open with its contents visible. The small amount of cash she had in it was partially exposed in a wrinkled envelope and unprotected. Standing there in utter disbelief, I thought that even a burglar with compromised eyesight would have no difficulty finding a key that he didn't need.

Eventually, even though her cognition remained intact and she tenaciously attempted to remain independent in her apartment, I noticed several deteriorative changes in her motor behavior. One that was obvious was a consistent anxious repetitive motion of her fingers that occurred while she was sitting at the table following a meal. She would scrape stray crumbs of bread into neat little mounds before sweeping them into a napkin with her palm. At other times, her arthritic fingers mimicked a chorea-like dance as she tore pieces from a paper napkin and twisted the corners into tortured points before placing them neatly on the table.

Sadly, these movements became progressively more obvious and exaggerated. When I think of that behavior, I am comforted when I remember that she occupied many hours during the day making delicate paper cherry ornaments for the Greek church bazaar for many years, and perhaps that constructive activity was a contributing factor in reducing her restlessness. Eventually, following the death of many of her contemporaries, she lost a purpose in life until the arrival of her great-grandchildren, who became a source of renewed energy for her.

Like many Greeks, my mother prearranged her funeral despite my consistent protestations. I am not exactly sure why she did that; perhaps it gave her a sense of security, knowing that her instructions would be carried out exactly. I attempted to reassure her on countless occasions that I would carry out her requests without exclusion, but she replied that she didn't want me to worry about the specifics.

In addition to the cash that she had so securely hidden in that small metal box in the closet were meticulous details regarding the arrangements she had made. Included were such specifics as what restaurant should host the Markaria meal following the Trisagion service and who should be invited, the amount to be donated to the Church, how much should be given to the priest for his services, and how much to tip the hairdresser. The list continued with such intricate detail that I was astonished. Further, she prearranged for a specific type of limousine and planned to have fur-covered chairs at the grave if the funeral was in the winter.

When she died at age ninety-nine, few of her contemporaries were still living, and the entire family fitted into a stretch limousine. Further, she died in the summer, but nonetheless, her request for fur-covered chairs at the grave was fulfilled! I know she would have laughed if she could have seen that sight.

I never realized that cleaning out my mother's apartment following her death would become such a daunting challenge. Initially, I didn't know where to start. Simply stated, and to my disbelief, sadly, my mother had become a hoarder. Without any great difficulty, I found paper bags, ribbons, old newspapers, and wrapping paper stuffed under the bed, behind her dresser, and in the metal closet. She had clearly thrown nothing away and begun accumulating everything.

Moreover, I discovered small amounts of cash that she had hidden in various areas within the apartment. She had money hidden between her mattress and the box spring, behind a mirror in her bedroom, exposed in a table drawer next to her recliner by the window, pinned to her brassiere in a dresser drawer, and even in the freezer compartment of the refrigerator. This practice, from my experience with older relatives, appears to come with aging, at least Greek aging. What were those old Greeks thinking? Sad but endearing, and a method, I imagine, of ensuring their security. (Oh God, I have a few dollars hidden under a shoe and covered by a shoe tree in my closet. I have become one of them.) I thank my mother for giving me life so that I can love my family.

My Father

Typically, Greek fathers know everything! They work hard, love their families, and strategize methods to keep their children close. Perhaps this represents a selfish motive, to some degree, in that they can eventually enjoy their grandchildren, participate in their development, and convince them to remain close to the family. "Oh those Greeks!"

Greek men who came from Greece generally married when they were older and more established, and they customarily married younger Greek women. That was the case with my father. From that perspective, we never thought it was unusual for our fathers to die when we were in our twenties. Not only did it produce an emptiness in our lives and deprive us of role models, but also our fathers were deprived of seeing us develop as adults, and even more important, many of them did not live long enough to love their grandchildren. However, in that era, it was the Greek way, and we had to accept it.

Because he worked two jobs and died at a relatively young age while I was still in graduate school, my father unfortunately never had extended discussions with me about his life in Greece.

My father had a distinct Greek accent, and his pronunciation of certain words made me smile. To this day, I often think, *If I could only hear my dad speak one more time.* But in a sense I can, because God has bestowed within all of us the most incredible gift—our memory. Whenever I choose, I can close my eyes, visualize him, and hear him speak. "And if you can't see me when my time is up, that means you are not trying hard enough!" As an example,

FAMILY

whenever we traveled to the White Mountains, a place that he loved perhaps because it reminded him of his home in Greece, he would talk about the "grizzles" that meandered through the woods. Grizzles? What in the world are grizzles? And who would know what he was talking about? But of course, I knew immediately. "Grizzles" are Greek for grizzly bears.

My father looked like a typical Greek, if that analogy exists. He had a slight frame with large brown eyes that twinkled through oversized, black-framed glasses that were too large for his face and were precariously supported by his Greek nasal hump. His silver hair was partially hidden by his hallmark, an old brownish gray fedora hat that he always wore pulled down, partially covering his eyes, whenever he left the house. The only time he didn't wear his hat this way was when he was playing cards in the kafenion, and then his hat was tilted upward, exposing his forehead, probably enabling him to see the cards better. He always wore a white shirt with a bowtie, poorly creased baggy pants, and an oversized, stretched-out old brown woolen sport coat with a cigar in the left vest pocket and a newspaper jammed into its stretched-out right pocket. After all, he was the advertising manager for the regional Greek newspaper, *The Acropolis*. To ensure he could provide for us, he also worked at night as a cashier at the Rockingham Race Track in Salem, New Hampshire.

Despite a blood dyscrasia that he contracted in his seventies, he continued to work, never complained while he was receiving debilitating treatments, and reluctantly retired only when he was too sick to continue. Whenever he had an opportunity to attend my high school baseball games, he would sit inconspicuously in a vacant corner of the stands with his legs crossed and, of course, with his newspaper jammed into his sport coat pocket. I remember one occasion, before the start of a game, when one of my friends saw him and said to me, "I think there is a professional baseball scout in the stands! He's got a paper, and he may be taking notes." I looked at my friend and then at my father and laughed. "Baseball scout? That's my father! Moreover, he doesn't even understand the game!"

A traditional custom of Greeks from a mountainous section in Northern Greece is to roast a lamb on a spit over an open fire. My father, coming from Lepinitsa in the northern mountains of Greece, loved to return to the mountains and enjoyed roasting lamb on a spit over an outdoor fire.

Occasionally in the summer, my father would buy small pieces of lamb from the butcher shop, garnish them with olive oil, oregano, garlic, and salt, and let them marinate overnight. The next day, usually a Sunday, we would pick up one or two of my aunts and drive for approximately one hour to a picnic area in the White Mountains of New Hampshire, where we would enjoy an outing.

Naturally, we could have barbecued the skewered lamb and eaten it at home, but it was my father's desire to go back to the mountains, and although we never talked about it at any great length, I am sure that it reminded him of his home in Northern Greece. In addition, it was a break from the city routine, and I think this might also have been a significant factor.

The location that he loved was so remote and secluded from the highway that I don't know how he ever found it in the first place. Furthermore, I wondered who would come to our assistance in the event of an emergency, since there were no cell phones or GPS units in those days, and I didn't see any public pay phones in the area. Even more worrisome, I wondered what would happen if a curious bear in the area smelled the lamb roasting and approached the open fire for an appetizer.

After we parked the car and emptied our provisions, and as we geared up to enter the woods and struggle awkwardly over that rocky trail, I had an unnerving feeling that someone or something was watching us. If that was the case, then whoever or whatever was scrutinizing us undoubtedly must have been amused as we prepared to trudge through a tortuous path leading to the picnic area. Assuming the role of a kleftes, a fifteenth-century mountain fighter and anti-Ottoman insurgent, my father led us up a narrow, muddy, rocky path that began as a gentle ascent into the woods. I laughed, because I thought that, instead of kleftes, we resembled Sherpas carrying food and other supplies on a mountain trek into the Himalayas. Any similarities ended quickly, however. Rather than sure-footed Sherpas, or the steady footed Evzones, the mountain fighters of Northern Greece, we looked more like a group of unsteady novices embarking on an uncertain goal.

The hike was not difficult for me, but it had to be strenuous for my mother and my aunts, who wore their customary long mourning dresses and heavy black shoes. Sneakers and slacks or shorts would have been more appropriate but were not part of a respectable Greek woman's wardrobe, regardless of the conditions. In retrospect, I shudder to think of what would have happened during one of those adventures if my mother or my aunt had stumbled while they were stepping over those rocks in their clumsy shoes and sprained or fractured an ankle. It would have resulted in chaos, and I couldn't imagine how we would have gotten them back to the car. Nevertheless, despite my concern, we pressed on, entered the trail, and began our expedition. I knew we were hiking toward the west, because it was early afternoon, and after a short distance in, the sun was blotted out by the tall pine trees and the mountain in front of us. Mercifully, after a short distance, the path suddenly ended, exposing a clearing with a weathered picnic table, a cluster of rocks arranged in a circle designating a fire pit, and countless numbers of voracious mosquitoes.

I couldn't imagine that he had chosen this location merely for the fire pit and the mosquitoes. Of course not! He had selected it, as many Greeks did and continue to do, for a specific reason. Proceeding westerly beyond the picnic area farther into the woods for a short distance, the gradual incline in the rocky terrain abruptly transformed into a vertical rocky ledge. Jutting out of that ledge was a pipe approximately three feet high embedded into the rock, from which flowed the clearest, coldest water conceivable. We congregated around that pipe like euphoric pixies dancing in the bright sunlight, drinking the water, and at the same time filling several jugs that we took home.

My father, ecstatic that we had reached our goal, jubilantly informed us of several mountain streams in Northern Greece, which had water that flowed with remarkable health benefits. My impression of that picnic area and its mountain stream remains as clear to me today as if I had been there yesterday. Events such as these brought great pleasure to my father, who otherwise worked tirelessly with two jobs so that I could get a college education and have a better life.

Since that time, I've returned to that stream only once to fill several bottles of water for him when he was seriously ill, but other than that, I have not gone back to that pipe in the mountain, because it was his special place and he would not be there. Nonetheless, I know he would like me to carry on the tradition, and perhaps one day I will hike into that picnic area in the New Hampshire woods with my grandchildren and create new memories. That would be wonderful, and it would complete the circle.

My father also loved the ocean, and whenever we went to the beach, he would exclaim, "We are returning to our place!" The only problem with that statement was that he came from a small village in the mountains of Northern Greece. But he felt that the ocean was his home, and I have found that most Greeks feel this way.

Most Greeks of my father's era were certain that the salty ocean water was therapeutic for all maladies, and my father was no exception. I still laugh as I visualize him floating on his back in the cold New Hampshire "therapeutic salt water." But he was back to the sea! Frequently in the summer we would drive to Hampton Beach, New Hampshire, an hour from our home, and visit my aunt Harriet (Χαρικλια), who owned a cottage one block from the shore.

My father had a passion for convertibles and referred to them as open cars. One afternoon, we test-drove an Austin Healy sprite convertible sports car, and he excitedly drove into our driveway honking the horn. I don't think we were there for more than a minute, but as soon as my mother came out and saw the car, his wide grin quickly turned into a disappointed frown, and we quickly backed out of the driveway and were on our way back to the dealer.

When my father developed blood dyscrasia, and when his condition progressed to the point where he was unable to work, we cared for him at home. He must have had a premonition one morning that he was going to die that day, because he directed me to have my mother buy a new black dress. It is

FAMILY

Greek tradition that women wear black for at least one year following a death in the family. As difficult as it was for me, I convinced her to go by reassuring her that his condition would remain unchanged until she returned. He told me it would be better if she weren't at home with us, and shortly after she left with my aunt, he died with me at his side.

What unfolded in the minutes following my father's death was absolute chaos, even by Greek standards. I telephoned the funeral director, who was a friend of mine, and before I knew it, and before my mother returned, the hearse drove in and parked in the middle of the driveway. Horrified, I ran out screaming that my mother was still away from home, and if she returned while the hearse was there, they would have two to contend with. Realizing the desperate situation and without hesitation, the driver of the hearse quickly left and parked around the corner until I called him again. Can you imagine what the neighbor must have been thinking when he saw the hearse in front of his home?

At the time of my father's death, a wake traditionally lasted two days and was held in a funeral home. And once again, as with any Greek event, despite its somber significance at first, it became a social event with food, pastries, and coffee available. In a typical custom, the casket was placed on a stand at the end of a large viewing room surrounded by bouquets of flowers, and for the first part of the evening, people filed by and paid their respects. Soon, however, individuals began to congregate into small groups and converse reservedly, and except for an occasional glance, the deceased was completely ignored.

During the wake, certain formalities had to be respected, and they usually occurred in an ordered sequence. In addition to the shrieking mourners, whose presence was obvious during the entire wake, if the deceased was a member of the AHEPA or the Macedonians (Greek social organizations), representatives of those organizations arrived to recite a brief prayer. Finally, the priest would arrive to recite a short prayer.

The formalities having been completed, the men would inconspicuously depart into a smaller adjoining room, where liquor quickly became available. In typical Greek tradition, the wake was transformed into a social event. By the end of the evening, it was not unusual to see several men, displaying a kyphotic posture reminiscent of a mischievous child being escorted to the bedroom, ushered out by their wives. Shortly after the wake began, my uncle Al arrived from Pennsylvania, and before I realized what was happening, we were standing in the funeral home's parking lot with his car's trunk open. Without any words being exchanged, he handed me a beer. It was his way of extending his love and comfort—that was my uncle Al.

For some reason, whenever I hear the song "Mr. Bojangles," and before I turn off the volume, I have a melancholy moment, because I think of my father, who ungrudgingly went without much for most of his life so that I could have more. But then again, that's the Greek way. Despite the memories rekindled by that song, I manage to elicit a smile, and I still can hear him turn to me and say, "My boy" (μου).

Greek Grandfathers

Grandfathers are the family patriarchs, the family advisors, and historians. Greek grandfathers generally wear the traditional Greek fisherman's hat, are able to drink considerable amounts of ouzo with no deleterious effects, and do not hesitate to remind family members, especially grandchildren, that they came to America with no money and worked hard. Greek grandfathers ensure that their grandchildren will receive a proper education and continue to emphasize that they "should be proud that they are Greek." Indisputably, grandfathers and grandchildren share a special bond.

I never met my grandfather on my father's side, since he never came to the United States. My grandfather on my mother's side, whose name was Christos, papou (παπου) to us, was a tall man and a former palace guard, an Evzone, in the Greek army. He lived with my mother's younger sister, my aunt Dora, on the third floor of an old neglected tenement on Cedar Street, in the Greek section of town directly across from the Assumption Greek Church.

As a young man, he was six feet three inches tall. As he aged, he became progressively more fragile, bent over, and debilitated by a hard life. Although he had a sunken face and was almost totally blind, his piercing blue eyes shined through cataract-obscured lenses. He utilized a cane to stabilize a severely unsteady, festinating gait, and on occasion he swung the cane wildly, as if attempting to deliver thunderbolts to anyone in his path. Although ouzo, with its distinct licorice flavor, was his favorite beverage, he eagerly drank any alcoholic beverage until the day he died at 102 years old.

Because of his cantankerous nature, my other cousins remained hesitant and never developed a relationship with him, visiting him only on rare occasions and on holidays. Perhaps because I was the oldest of the grandchildren living locally, I would visit him regularly, and we would sit on that deteriorating third-floor porch that overlooked the Greek church and Greek bakery on one side of the street and the litter-strewn alley in the back while he rocked in his creaky rocker in the afternoon sunshine.

Periodically, when he was comforted by the warm afternoon sunlight and he felt well enough, the strain on his face moderated, and he became animated and began to describe his life and adventures in Greece—mostly in Greek but partly in English. Occasionally he would surprise me by expressing an opinion regarding current world affairs and politics, but most of the time we would just sit together silently while he rocked peacefully.

Despite Christos being severely visually impaired, I had the sense from his facial expressions that in his mind he could still clearly visualize elements of his life in Greece. He was a proud man of a different era, and when he died, my family and the Hellenic Republic lost an evzone. The years fall as do the swallows (Πεφτανε τα χρονια σαν τα χελιδονια). I have always considered myself fortunate to have been exposed to three generations of a Greek family.

Greek Grandmothers

A Greek grandmother may appear to be unyielding on the outside, but as many of you know from experience, she is full of love. As a matter of fact, she may be overprotective to the point where she may become oppressive. Furthermore, she will swiftly make you feel guilty when you behave badly or when she becomes disappointed by your actions for some reason. In those latter instances, and for no apparent logical reason, she will be likely to exclaim, "I will die, and I will die soon!" Obviously, this is an attempt to instill guilt.

When a Greek grandmother is not living with her grandchildren and feels as though she doesn't see them enough, she cannot avoid imparting guilt when she does see them. As an example of this behavior, if a granddaughter were to mention that she liked a piece of her grandmother's jewelry, her grandmother's response might likely be, "You can have it when I die." Again, this is an attempt to ensure a timely return visit. If I told my grandmother I was coming to see her soon, she would reply, "I hope you are coming before I die" or, "If I am not dead by then."

Moreover, a Greek grandmother is more than likely to ask a newlywed couple, "When are you going to have children? I want to see them before I die." Despite these domineering qualities, and the exceptional ability to infuse guilt, a Greek grandmother provides a protected environment of abounding love and care.

Greek grandmothers occupy a prominent position within the Greek family, and it seemed natural that they were supposed to be living with you. Unfortunately, I never knew my grandmothers, since they both died before I was born, depriving me of the opportunity to live in a home with three generations of females, and I envied my friends who had grandmothers. Grandmothers, in addition to providing endless love, contribute to the stability of the family and provide a sense of security and comfort for their grandchildren. They seemed to always be there.

Luckily for me, the Greeks have an answer for everything, including an apparent grandmother scarcity. One of the assets of our culture is that there are many Greek women who are ready to assume the role of surrogate grandmothers.

Of the eligible candidates in my extended family when I was younger, the most likely choice was my aunt Harriet. She and my mother's mother were sisters, and she was more than eager to accept the role and the assignment of helping to bring me up to be an obedient Greek American child. As a matter of fact, she thought it was her duty to do so. She was married to Uncle Bill, a retired diner owner, and they had three grown children, Cecile, Florence, and Chris.

In contrast to most Greeks who lived in the Greek section, my aunt Harriet and uncle Bill owned a well-maintained, three-family tenement home with a manicured lawn and several flowering bushes located on the city's north side on a street lined by stately elm trees. They had a large front porch with a heavy brown wooden door and an opaque oval window. I remember sitting on their sun-drenched front porch in the fall and watching the leaves fall from the trees that lined the street on either side. I can't explain the significance of that image and why I continue to retain it, but it is fascinating how the mind captures and retains selected childhood memories. Perhaps it was because the street where I lived had no trees.

They occupied the first floor with their two daughters, Florence and Cecile, while their son, Chris, and his wife, Elefkothea, and their three young sons, Bill, Anthony, and Michael, lived on the third floor. Following Greek tradition, Bill, the oldest son, was named for his paternal grandfather.

Being part of the extended family, we would visit them three to four times a week on a regular basis. Outwardly, my aunt appeared to be a stern lady—tall and thin, with silver hair tightly wrapped into a bun that accentuated her sharp nose. I remember that she always wore either a gray or black dress with heavy black shoes and black stockings knotted just below the knees. She walked with a conspicuous limp due to a severely arthritic hip, but despite that disability, she maintained an imposing posture that allowed her to accelerate her pace rapidly within a moment's notice.

Her weapon of choice, as she was pursuing me and my disobedient Macedonian warrior cousins through her home, was a large wooden spoon that she withdrew from her apron at the waist. She could manage it with authority, and it was especially effective when used across the buttocks with calculated strokes accompanied by specific phrases, such as, "Now over here, over there, again over here! Here! Here!" (τωρα απο εδω, απο εκει, παλη απο εδω, να, να, να!)

Although it was uncomfortable, it was amusing to watch her struggle as she went through that ritual with her stern face and pursed lips. Another of her favorite expressions was, "I broke my spoon; now I'm going to have to kill you!" (Εσπασα το κουταλα μου τωρα πρεππει να σε σκοτωσω!) These expressions would strike fear into our hearts, and we quickly determined that the most effective way to avoid the wooden spoon was to avoid trouble and, if that wasn't possible, to run and seek sanctuary under the bed. I can still visualize lying under the bed and staring at her long, thin, bowed legs covered by black nylon stockings as we listened to the punishment that awaited us as disobedient Macedonian warriors as soon as we were captured.

My aunt Harriet performed her matriarchal duties with dignity and respect, and she was always there for me. She was in her late eighties when I was a teenager, but she was still a Fury. Her vitality allowed her to successfully overcome a hip fracture at age ninety-one, and she recovered rapidly and completely from a total hip replacement at age ninety-two. Because of her stern disposition, many of my cousins and friends felt uncertain when they were in her presence, and even my wife, after she met Aunt Harriet for the first time prior to our marriage, remained tentative. Nonetheless, my aunt was a loving and devoted grandmother to me, and she was always there for me.

I was also fortunate to have a second surrogate grandmother. She was my best friend Louie's grandmother. Unlike my aunt Harriet, she was diminutive and appeared to be fragile. She had an exaggerated kyphotic posture, hollow cheeks, prominent cheekbones, a large nose with a Grecian bump, and salt-and-pepper hair knotted in a bun atop her head, making her look like a Greek witch.

Given these characteristics, however, when you were in her presence, you would spontaneously focus on her bright, large brown piercing eyes. As with most Greek widows, she always wore the typical black mourning outfit. Her especially thin, frail-appearing legs were supported by black stockings, the latter of course knotted just below the knees to further constrict the circulation to the legs.

Looks can be deceiving, and in this case dangerous, because despite her fragile appearance, she was likely to break into a frenzy at a moment's notice if provoked. As a matter of fact, I remember her on several occasions chasing Louie's younger brother through the house with her dreaded wooden spoon, and for that reason, Louie and I were always careful not to incite her. In concert with the phrase that the young do not listen to the old, the Greeks have a saying, "My grandmother says something, and my ears hear something else." (Αλλα λεει η γιαγια μου, αλλα ακουν τα αυτια.)

Typical of Greek grandmothers, whenever we were at Louie's home, his grandmother would insist that we eat, whether we were hungry or not. I will always remember the delicious χωριατικι (peasant salad usually made with onions, cucumbers, tomatoes, feta cheese, oil, and love) that she made and how quickly she made it. Two of my other close friends didn't have grandparents either, and we always seemed to congregate at Louie's home—most likely because there was always something there for us to eat.

Despite their frequent frenzies, grandmothers provide comfort and inspiration from the daily routines and the lifelong habits by handing down their unconditional love, family values, history, and traditions. They provide their grandchildren with a sense of stability, and although I never had the opportunity to experience that directly, I perceive and appreciate that sense of comfort in my grandchildren when they are with their grandmother. Through her constant attention and recurrent affectionate embraces, and the smiles on their faces, my grandchildren know that they are secure.

Οικογενεια: The Family

How is this term defined by Greeks? Does it include the parents, children, grandparents, relatives, and friends? Typically, to the Greeks, the extended family is considered the basic family unit where all members take part in discussions, decisions, and daily operations. An expression that is predictably Greek is, "Welcome! If you are Greek, you are family." (Καλως ηλθατε, αν ειστε Ελληνες, ειστε οικογενεια!) This expression characterizes both my parents' families.

My mother's family consisted of an aggregate of colorful personalities. The only commonality they shared, other than their surname, was that they were all loving individuals. Other than that, well, perhaps I can relate some of their uniqueness to you. My mother had four sisters, in descending ages—Victoria, Ourania (but we called her Nia), Dora, and Kelly—and two brothers, George and Alex, and as in any Greek family, you could sense the closeness and love they had for each other, even though heated discussions and arguments among them were common.

My mother's younger brother, Uncle Al, was a steelworker, and his large stature was exceeded only by the size of his heart. He reminded me of a giant, gentle, cuddly teddy bear. He was married to my aunt Margie, a non-Greek woman, who was affectionate and accepted by our family without reservation. They had three daughters, Donna, Sharon, and Nancy.

Because of few improving employment opportunities in Manchester, they eventually relocated to Pennsylvania, where my uncle became employed in the steel factories. Despite numerous trips to their home in Pennsylvania, I could sense that the geographical distance affected the sibling relationship.

My mother's older brother, Uncle George, lived in Boston and was a railroad conductor for the Boston and Maine Railroad. He had a daughter named Kay, who was the oldest of the first cousins. I always sensed that he was the most independent of my mother's siblings and quite a flamboyant character. He promised me on several occasions that he would take me to a baseball or basketball game in Boston, but we never made it. Whenever he would see me, he would say, "I haven't forgotten, and we will go to a game soon." Although we never went, and I sensed we never would, I knew his intentions were sincere, and I loved him.

My uncle George's second wife, Agnes, who was not Greek, did not appear to be the most affectionate person and absolutely did not want anything to do with our family. Initially, I wondered if she felt overwhelmed by our family, but despite repeated attempts to include her, she preferred to exclude us.

One day, after arranging a compatible time to visit their brother George, my aunts drove to his home in Boston. No sooner had the car stopped in front of his apartment than Agnes poked her head out of the second-floor window and curtly informed them that George wasn't home. She then abruptly closed the window, and that was the end of that. She never reappeared, and the bewildered sisters drove back to New Hampshire. I would have loved to have been a fly on the wall during that trip, because I can just imagine the temperament of their conversation on the drive home. It's a good thing Greeks do not carry grudges! What? On the contrary! They refused to see Agnes again.

My mother was very close to her sisters, and most family social interactions, as far as I can remember, involved them. My mother's oldest sister, Victoria, married a non-Greek, Uncle Pete, from Boston, Massachusetts. They lived in a large brown Victorian home with their daughter Judy, who is four years older than me, in the Blue Hills section of Wollaston, Massachusetts—a lovely residential area inundated with many large trees adjacent to a golf course.

Unlike her other sisters, and perhaps in response to occupational requirements as a beautician, Victoria was more attentive to well-styled hair and dressed in chic designs. When I was younger, I thought she was fortunate to have escaped from the Greek community, but in retrospect, her other sisters were more fortunate, because they stayed together and retained their Greekness. We did, however, remain close to her family, and reciprocal visits occurred frequently. I am still close with my cousin Judy. Whenever I smell burning leaves, I am transported back to those visits to my aunt Victoria's home when my cousin Judy and I would jump into leaf piles before they were burned.

My aunt Ourania (Nia) lived approximately three miles from us in a newly built, attractive, compact yellow Cape Cod house atop a steep hill overlooking the city. The house had a small sunroom in front with large windows on three sides that delivered ample sunlight, provided warmth, and offered a view of the city below and the mountains beyond it in the distance. Her home, surrounded by Greek neighbors, their yards complete with grape trellises and of course a space reserved for vegetable and flower gardens, could be considered a microcosm of Greekness.

Like my father, my aunt Nia's husband, Uncle John, would spend countless hours sitting in his garden watering and talking to his tomatoes, coercing them to ripen. In the evenings during the week, we would frequently visit my aunt Nia, and usually every Friday evening, the sisters would gather at her house for a spaghetti supper. Those remain wonderful memories and are a testament to the integrity of the extended Greek family.

To supplement my uncle John's income, my aunt Nia had an industrial shoe-stitching machine in her basement that enabled her to stitch shoes that were delivered to her on consignment from the shoe factories. I remember the basement floor would flood with several inches of water following heavy rainstorms. Despite that, my aunt continued to stitch, and I was amazed she wasn't electrocuted.

My uncle John owned and operated the Empire Diner in town prior to his retirement. Like many Greek diner owners, he did it all—he was the cook, dishwasher, and cashier. Eventually, his retirement was facilitated by the physical difficulties of the job, as well as the persistent insistence of retired Greek neighbors who, in addition to talking to their tomato plants as well, would congregate and discuss the good old days.

Unfortunately, however, one of the adverse but inevitable consequences of aging in many instances is that decision making is affected. Once, while my aunt was at the supermarket and my uncle John was left home alone, a kitchenware salesman came to the door and eagerly displayed his products to my unwary uncle, who, being a former restaurant owner, and perhaps thinking at that moment that he was still in business, listened intently and enthusiastically purchased over $500 worth of pots and pans, certainly not a trivial amount in those days. The deal was completed and presumably forgotten until later that month when the salesman reappeared with the kitchenware and the bill.

This time, however, when the salesman arrived, circumstances were quite different. My aunt, who was unaware of the previous transaction, greeted the salesman at the door. At the threshold, blocking any further entry, she stood—a stout, robust woman, no taller than five feet, her hair pulled back into a bun, her checkered black-and-white dress extending just below the knees, exposing her knotted nylon brown stockings, her apron tightly cinched at her waist with a wooden spoon tucked into the waist strap, and her hands on her hips—a daunting figure ready for battle.

Sensing a potential problem, the salesman warily advised my aunt of the previous transaction that my uncle had agreed to. Without further delay, she ordered him sternly and in no uncertain terms to "tear up that contract and get those pots out of here!" She went on to exclaim forcefully, "My husband is a senior citizen, and he's not responsible for his actions!" At that point, bewildered and unwilling to be the loser in that confrontation, the salesman and his kitchenware hastily exited. I would have loved to have seen the expression on his face when my aunt confronted him.

My aunt Dora, the next-to-the-youngest sister, lived with my uncle John (yes, another Uncle John who shined shoes), their daughter Joyce, son Chris, and my grandfather who, as you know, was named Christos. They lived on the third floor of a large, run-down, weathered tenement building in the Greek section of town, directly across the street from one of the Greek churches.

Dora had a loving personality, but tragically, she became so morbidly obese later in life that she became unable to descend the stairs from her third-floor apartment and, for approximately ten years, became trapped in that space with no means of egress in the event of a fire or a life-threatening illness. But Dora never worried about those prospects, despite the family's constant attempts to persuade her. Finally, the family was relocated to another apartment, and she was carried precariously down three flights of stairs by six medical attendants and firemen. A few years later, she went to an assisted-living facility, was given a motorized scooter, and because of her exuberant personality, quickly became its unofficial social director.

Kelly (Kaliope), the youngest and most volatile sister, lived with my uncle Carroll, a non-Greek man in Epsom, New Hampshire, a rural village approximately thirty minutes from us, with their two sons, Leslie and Russell. Passionate, stubborn, opinionated, highly volatile, and even flammable on occasion, but always very loving, she embodied this family's very Greek characteristics. As I think about it, because of her fiery nature, it would have been more appropriate if she had been named Elektra rather than Kaliope. Even more intriguing, her husband, Carroll, had the most compliant temperament imaginable, supporting the saying that opposites attract.

My aunt Kelly and one or more of her sisters always seemed to have a conflict or at least friction between them, and usually they would not speak until the issue was forgotten. When she became excited, and it didn't take much to provoke her, the pitch of her voice would intensify to the point that it became piercing. Even so, she emanated warmth, and I always looked forward to seeing her. From my experience, this fiery characteristic appears to be to be a trait present in a number of Greeks. Perhaps this represents an edict from the Greek gods!

My aunt Kelly is currently the only surviving sister and has assumed the matriarchal role within the family. Now that she is a nonagenarian, and although she still displays rare periods of excitability, she has become more composed and at times seems passive and generally disinterested. She is an alarming example of the distressing fragmentation of the Greek community and the disintegration of the family unit. At her insistence to remain independent, she lives alone in municipal housing and currently has been relocated to a convalescent home.

I can never forget my uncle Louie Kosmas, my father's first cousin. He lived with his sister Stiliano in a tenement in the Greek section of Manchester. Uncle Louie's greatest physical characteristic was his hair. He couldn't have had more than one hundred silvery hairs on his head, but each one of them stood at perfect attention!

My uncle Louie's other sister, my aunt Mary, was a remarkable woman and a unique character in many respects. She married a Greek man, and her family moved to Idaho before I was born. Following the tragic death of her husband in an automobile accident in 1942, my father drove to Idaho to bring my aunt Mary and her seven children back to New Hampshire to reunite them with her family—further confirming the closeness of the extended Greek family.

Aunt Mary had four sons and three daughters in descending order of ages: Charlie, George, Ted, and Larry (Nappy), and Evangeline, Helen, and Peggy. Her sons served in the military during WWII. My uncles Ted and George were on the same battleship but were eventually separated by the navy to minimize the eventuality of their death from an attack. Fortunately, all the brothers returned safely from the war.

My dear aunt Mary was one of the most loving ladies and extremely fascinating personalities you could meet. Although her children all relocated to California, she remained in Manchester and lived on the third floor of an old tenement in the Greek section opposite one of the Greek markets and across the street from the Greek church. Conceivably because she left Greece as an adult and remained predominantly within the Greek community, as most Greeks of that generation did, she retained her heavy accent. She had an endearing custom of starting every sentence, regardless of its context, with, "You no see," which quickly became her hallmark.

She was also a compulsive soap opera fan. If someone happened to make an ill-timed ascent up three flights of stairs to her apartment when her favorite soap opera program was in progress, she would ignore them and would refuse to answer the door. It didn't make any difference who it was; they could have stood at that door all afternoon. I know, because it happened to me on several occasions—I was ignored by my own aunt. I would simply shake my head, shout to her that I would come later, and descend three flights of stairs, only to make another attempt later that day. Generally, however, due to my persistence, I was rewarded with a piece of baklava or spanakopita.

Later in her life, when I was in high school, Aunt Mary finally relocated to Southern California to be close to her children. She was a loving member of our family, and I missed her greatly.

An eccentric peculiarity that my aunt Mary had was that she would never buy prepared ground hamburger from the market. Instead, she would buy the beef and bring it home, where she ground it herself with a hand meat grinder. Her explanation for this unconventional behavior was that she didn't know "what was put in the meat grinder before her beef." One of the first things she asked her daughter after relocating to San Diego to be with her conjugate family was, "Do you have a meat grinder?"

Another amusing example of the conflict that existed between the retention of Greekness and the process of assimilation occurred when my father eventually visited my aunt Mary and her family in California. My aunt Mary and her daughter Evangeline (Vangy) drove to Los Angeles to pick him up at the airport, and they stopped to have dinner in a diner on the way to San Diego. When they finished eating, my aunt Mary asked for a doggie bag, and my father, who was always proper, told my aunt that to ask for a doggie bag was embarrassing. She looked at him incredulously but did not utter a word. When the waitress finally brought her the bag, my father exclaimed to the waitress with an obvious Greek accent, "It's for her dog, you know!"

My aunt Mary, in her heavy Greek accent quickly replied, "I'm the dog!"

My father became irate, and as they were leaving the restaurant, he turned to her and exclaimed in a firm voice, "And now you know why I always say that I am the Cosmas with the *C*! I tried to save you from embarrassment, but you wouldn't listen!"

I can almost hear the response from my aunt Mary and the tenor of the conversation between the two of them as they drove toward San Diego. And, of course, I could empathize with my aunt Vangy, who had to listen to them as she drove!

I SUPPOSE IF I HAD to choose a hero other than my father, who worked two jobs to provide me with opportunities that he never had, it would be my uncle Ted, my aunt Mary's son. He played football and baseball in college in New Hampshire and met his future wife June while they were in college. She was from Carlsbad, California, but after their graduation, they remained in New Hampshire and opened a restaurant following his career as a minor league pitcher. I remember that Uncle Ted would hit fly balls to me, so I could develop my baseball skills. Shortly thereafter, however, and for those of you who remember the song "California Dreaming," they were lured to Southern California, where they settled in an oceanside community north of San Diego where he became a successful developer. His relocation affected me greatly, since I had lost my role model. Many years passed before I saw him again, but eventually I flew to San Diego. The first thing we did when I arrived was to get out the baseball gloves and throw the ball around. For a brief period, our relationship was like it always was. My uncle Ted will always be my hero.

Godfathers

Godfathers are important figures in Greek life. They are considered part of the extended family and provide additional support for their godchildren. In the event that the parents become unable to care for the child, the godparents may be expected to step in and assist. They also have important roles in religious ceremonies and are considered integral members of the nuclear family. I remember my godfather's large home on the outskirts of Manchester that sat on a large tract of sun-drenched land overlooking a large, crystal-clear lake. It is interesting how specific images remain imprinted in our minds, and this one became prominent perhaps because his home represented such an extreme departure from the homes of Greeks that I knew who, like me, lived in neighborhoods where tenements were the norm and the homes were close to one another within the city limits. Whenever we visited my godparents, I wondered what it would be like to live there.

More significant, however, is my memory of my godfather and his occupation. He was a cobbler and owned a small shoe repair shop in Derry, New Hampshire, that I visited several times. Nonetheless, I would be remiss if I did not describe my first visit there to you, because that scene will always remain permanently imprinted in my memory, and it quite likely might reawaken some similar memories for you.

His cobbler shop was on the first floor of an old, gray, three-story wooden building squeezed between two other businesses located on a side street. The large, dirty front windows were partly covered by short, sun-faded brown curtains supported by brass curtain rods that obscured the light. The first thing you noticed as you entered his shop, in addition to the distinct scent of leather, was the low-hanging, discolored cream ornate metal ceiling that gave you the oppressive feeling that it was about to fall on you. It must have been the victim of years of cigarette and cigar smoke.

Typical of most shoe repair shops, the front retail area had counters and shoe repair equipment, as well as shoes in various stages of repair. As I cautiously walked between the repair tools, machinery, and counters toward the rear of the shop, a faded and tattered tan curtain separated the front retail area from the dark back room. Once, as I tentatively reached for the curtain and slowly opened it, staring into the dimly lit back room, my gaze involuntarily shifted to the ceiling area while I struggled to compensate for the dimness. I was astonished to see what appeared to be large, brown serpentine-like structures dangling sinuously from clothesline ropes hanging from the low ceiling and distributed throughout the entire back room. These creatures appeared ready to drop onto an unsuspecting prey. Initially horrified, I stood motionless for a few seconds before realizing with relief that, with assistance from my olfactory sense, they were sausages with leeks (λουκάνικο με πράσα) drying in their casings and not reptiles ready to pounce on me. As you can imagine, I will never forget that sight and can still visualize that shop with amazing clarity.

I HAVE GONE INTO RATHER elaborate detail to describe a typical Greek family as well as my immediate and extended Greek family, and you can see how inclusive the Greek family is. This portrayal has also been intended to remind us of the difficulties that our grandparents and parents encountered as immigrants while endeavoring to make life better for their families. Also, this characterization is my attempt to inform the newer generations of younger individuals what life was like for their immigrant families who came to this country. Our older generations struggled and did the best they could to provide for us in the best way they knew, hoping that the future would be easier for us.

We need to recognize and appreciate their efforts in attempting to improve their world for succeeding generations of Greeks, as well as non-Greeks. Many of our older relatives did not have the opportunity to receive a college education, but it was their aspiration that their children might, and they continued to work tirelessly to afford them that opportunity. I became the first in my family in my generation to receive a college education, and some of my cousins followed. The challenge has been handed off to us, and as children of immigrants, or not, we must continue to carry on these traditions and responsibilities so that our children and grandchildren will have a more secure life. We must do the best for our children with the expectation that they will do the same for theirs. After all, it's the Greek way.

CHAPTER 6

Growing Up Greek

"Remain young, my son, and you will forever be an Evzone"

THIS GREEK CULTURE BEGINS AT birth. If you are a boy, your first name is taken from your paternal grandfather, and your middle name from your father. If you are a girl, your first name is taken from your maternal grandmother, and your middle name from your mother. And then there is the extended family—parents, grandparents, uncles, aunts, cousins, and friends. The numbers become astronomical. And it becomes very difficult to explain this concept of "family" to your non-Greek friends. At least, it was when I was growing up. It would have been easier to explain that all the Greeks in town are "my family" rather than to stumble through a lengthy explanation that made no sense and have my friends look at me in bewilderment.

And then, of course, there's the Greek school. At the completion of the school day, my non-Greek friends went home to play outdoors. But this isn't what happened if you were Greek! Waiting for you outside the American school was either one of your parents or grandparents eager to transport you to the Greek school, where you would spend at least two hours learning how to read and write the Greek language as well as learning about culture and traditions. Religious education was generally reserved for the Sunday school that preceded a two-hour Sunday religious service. And that's not all. We were encouraged to join and attend a social club called GOYA (Greek Orthodox Youth Association) for pre-teens and teenagers that met during the evening on regular occasions and sponsored Greek dances and a basketball league. Those of you of my generation understand what I am describing. It was all Greek! This is "Greekness!"

Taking part of a quote from Elia Kazan, "I am a Greek by blood, a Turk by birth and an American because my uncle made the journey." When I was growing up, on first impression, perhaps because of my blue eyes and moderately fair complexion, people were astonished to learn that I was Greek, but I would quickly exclaim that I had blue eyes like Alexander the Great, King Leonidas, Achilles, and other ancient Greek heroes. My primary language was Greek, and we spoke that exclusively at home and whenever we visited relatives. I started to learn English only after entering kindergarten in the public grammar school when I was five years old, and that was an interesting experience for me, my teacher, and classmates.

When I began kindergarten, it was necessary for my mother to write several essential words in phonetic Greek, such as water (νερο) and bathroom (τουαλετα), so that my teacher, Ms. Gallagher, would understand. Nonetheless, with Ms. Gallagher's enduring patience and encouragement, I began to adapt and eventually became bilingual. It must have been mystifying for Ms. Gallagher, at least initially, to have a kindergartner who spoke only Greek and had a cloth talisman filled with garlic pinned to the inside of his pocket to avoid germs and ward off the evil eye! The simplicity of my kindergarten experience as well as those memories remain vivid, and Ms. Gallagher, the other students, and I persevered.

The House Where I Grew Up

When I was a child, we lived two miles outside the center of the city in an old, gray, shingled two-story single-family home on Shasta Street in a mixed ethnic neighborhood. Although I never asked, I believe this location was my father's attempt to remove us from downtown tenement life, and I am certain he was proud to be able to accomplish that.

Typical of most Greek homes of that vintage, at the end of a short cement driveway stood a grape trellis supported by unsteady rusty piping that provided succulent green grapes in the fall as well as a sweet aroma that permeated the entire area. Behind the trellis in an undersized fenced-in backyard was a mulberry tree and, of course, wedged into the right corner, a vegetable garden with tomatoes, peppers, and scallions protected by a rickety, discolored, off-white picket fence in disrepair that separated our yard from an old weathered brown wooden barn next door.

Positioned strategically in front of that garden was a small wobbly wooden chair, where my father would spend countless hours watering and talking to his tomato plants, coercing them to grow as he smoked his cigar. This is an endearing image that I will never forget. If I close my eyes, I can visualize walking up that cracked cement driveway and hearing my father in conversation. I expected he might have been talking with one of my uncles or aunts, but when I reached the backyard, I could see that he was alone in the garden and was simply convincing his tomato plants to grow more quickly while admonishing the cutworms. Next to the trellis, a short, decaying cement stairway led to a weathered, unsteady, red back door that opened into a small hallway. Beyond that was the kitchen, bathroom, pantry, dining room, and parlor.

A small solitary bathroom on the first floor satisfied the needs of the family. Typical of many old homes and tenements during those good old days, bathrooms were not equipped with showers, and the only option was the bathtub unless we were at the YMCA or the high school, where showers were available. That was the case in my home, but my friends and I planned to alter that deficiency. Instead of a shower, on the first floor, on the worn and uneven, old, cracked, vinyl-tiled bathroom floor, under a small window, protected by a weathered pink vinyl curtain, wedged intimately close to an archaic white chipped sink with corroded metal legs, stood an old white steel bathtub supported by four stubby legs.

Following an outdoor basketball game on a hot summer day, Louie, George, Chris—my three best friends growing up, who replaced the brothers I never had—and I decided that it would be a great idea to have a shower and that it should be installed at my home. It has finally become clear to me many years later why my home was chosen for the shower. Louie's grandmother was always home, as were Chris's and George's mothers, and they would have flatly rejected the project. My parents, however, were working, so there would be no opposition. We proceeded with our plan and purchased a shower kit from Moreau's Hardware Store that consisted of a metal support that screwed into the wall to hold a shower head, and a four-foot square metal supportive ring from which hung a flimsy white vinyl curtain. Extending from the showerhead, a long brown rubber hose took a sinuous pathway that ultimately attached insecurely to the bathtub faucet. Ecstatic that we had successfully completed our construction project, the four of us lined up to take a shower. I can still see their faces as we stood there with great anticipation, each waiting impatiently for his turn. This is a sight I will never forget! Despite the leaks at the faucet, Shasta Street had a shower.

Beyond the kitchen was a large, black, circular, ornate metal grate placed strategically in the floor between the dining room and the parlor to supply the house with heat from a coal-burning furnace, which was eventually replaced by a newer duct-heating system that utilized oil. Prior to that, when heat was required, my father would shovel coal into the furnace from a pile of coal adjacent to it.

The furniture in the parlor consisted of a sofa and two armchairs wrapped in clear, thick vinyl to protect the upholstery that no one was permitted to sit on. Those of you from my era know exactly what I'm talking about. Furthermore, as you remember, if you tried to sit on the sofa or either of the armchairs, the prospects were excellent that you would slide right off because of the slippery plastic covers. And doilies were strategically placed where a person's head and arms would rest. Embroidered doilies were everywhere in Greek homes—on tabletops, on the back of reclining armchairs, on shelves, and on pillows. To put the finishing touches on the room, a small, wooden coffee table separated the sofa from the chairs. I used to call this the "look-at" room, because the only times it was used was when a physician was making a house call, when a priest was blessing the home, or when relatives that we hadn't seen for months were visiting. To a Greek, all of this makes perfect sense! From the parlor, a narrow stairway led to three small sparingly furnished bedrooms on the second floor. Since mine had a western exposure, it was bright, and the afternoon sun warmed it nicely.

One of my most vivid memories of our old house was its damp, gloomy, shadowy, rock-lined basement. It was an eerie place, to say the least, and its entry from the dim back-hallway staircase might be analogous to a descent into the underworld. If you had enough courage, and after successfully negotiating the dark, narrow wooden stairway, you entered the world of Hades, the entry of which was protected by an old washing machine and sink. To the right of the washer, ropes were suspended from the wooden beams to be used as a clothesline, which obscured vision even further. Beyond that point, and lurking deeper within the darkness, loomed a large, oil-burning furnace, which had replaced its coal-burning predecessor. With its numerous ducts extending from the main trunk, the furnace reminded me of Medusa enticing any trespasser who had entered the underworld.

Our house was directly across the street from a large junkyard enclosed by a high barbed-wire fence. Inside were numerous old automobile wrecks and twisted, sharp pieces of metal and glass that provided a dangerous environment for foolish young children to explore. Recognizing the potential danger, the neighbors eventually assembled and petitioned for its removal, and it was finally cleaned up and converted into a sandlot playground. When I was about nine years old, the junkyard was cleared, and the vacant sandlot suddenly became a baseball field inundated with young baseball players honing their skills and utilizing taped broken bats and old baseballs that had been beaten coverless and wrapped in black electrical tape. A few of the ballplayers had baseball gloves, and some of us used old, worn garden gloves, but we played ball!

Although I didn't know it at that time, my exit from the Greek section years later might have been assisted by the sandlot games and by a large weathered telephone pole that stood across the street from our house. I consistently threw rocks from our driveway at that pole, attempting to cut down any runner trying to steal second base. I think that's how I began to develop what little skill I had as a baseball player.

As I became older and began to play organized baseball, my mother was always in attendance, supporting me and cheering loudly in the stands. Well, except for one occasion that I will never forget, which still makes me laugh whenever I think of it. I was a catcher, but during this game, the coach asked me to pitch, since we were being beaten badly and running out of pitchers. As I walked to the mound, I heard a commotion in the stands. It was my mother, standing and screaming, "Don't let him pitch. He'll kill someone!" I looked up, laughed, and said to myself, "Atta girl, Mom, that's great parental support!"

Since there were no school buses when I was in elementary school, we walked to school in the morning, came home for lunch, and walked back for the afternoon session. Life was less complex in those days, and safety was not as great an issue. Typically, when the school day concluded in midafternoon, my life differed greatly from my non-Greek friends. While they were going home to play outdoors, much to my consternation, I was picked up by my father and driven directly to the Greek school for three hours of Greek lessons. I can't say that I loved that part of the day.

The Greek School

The Greek school had different classes, and my class had approximately ten students, in contrast to the twenty students in my class in the public school in Manchester. The public school had large windows that provided more than adequate sunlight. Further, brightly colored posters hung everywhere, and the walls were covered with brilliant student-colored pictures, creating a cheerful environment. The Greek school, however, was more typical of a Spartan environment—dreary and stark, with only the necessary furniture, equipment, and materials necessary to teach the students the elements of Greek. On either side of the narrow, dimly lit corridor on the second floor of the Hellenic Community Center were drab classrooms, each equipped with old, dark brown wooden desks and chairs bolted to the floor. The gloomy atmosphere, enhanced by the stark, gray walls devoid of bright posters or drawings of animals or happy children dancing, was interrupted only at the front by the teacher's desk. Behind that, a chalkboard, a Greek flag, and a picture of the stern, staring archbishop hung on the wall. Most likely because of the vintage of this building, as well as its closeness to the tenement next door, the absence of classroom windows created a confining environment, making it impossible to determine what time of day it was.

Greek school was more formal than public school. Subjects included reading, writing, vocabulary, Greek history, culture, mythology, and proper behavior. Greek school teachers had greater autonomy and were stricter and more authoritative, and they were reinforced by the priest, who was usually in his office ready to intercede if a disciplinary problem required his attention. God help the ill-fated student whose parents received a phone call from the teacher or, even worse, from the priest, but I don't remember this ever happening to me.

Mrs. A., our teacher, was a short, stern buxom lady, who wielded a twenty-four-inch ruler with a metal edge and was quite capable of managing any situation. Whenever she walked over those uneven wooden classroom floors, the pounding of her thick-heeled shoes sent chills up your spines. Moreover, if you hadn't prepared your assignment or were reluctant to recite it, she would loom over you, and as the thick, black hairs that extended from her chin became more prominent, she became more terrifying. Does any of this sound familiar to you? She must have been a descendant of Athena, the goddess of war. And further, if I went home and told my parents that Mrs. A. had reprimanded me, they, without question or hesitation, would reinforce her actions. From my observations, it doesn't appear that we have quite the same concept of proper behavior, behavior modification, and respect in our current society. I cannot articulate how grateful I am that my parents required me to attend Greek school and complete my Greek education, even though it seemed like torture then.

March 25th, Greek Independence Day, is a day of jubilant celebration for Greeks and a day all of us kids at Greek school dreaded. Greek Independence Day represents the beginning of the war for independence from Ottoman Turkey and not the actual independence, the epanastasis (τουρκροκρατια). It continues to represent a day of celebration for the Greeks, marked by parades and, yes, with anxious schoolchildren dressed in authentic costumes reciting poems and dancing on stages everywhere.

Despite its national significance, it was a day of extreme anxiety for many of us in my Greek school class, because certain students would be selected to memorize a poem and recite it on stage in front of the community. I was selected to be one of those evzones, and I agonized for weeks to commit a poem to memory, and just when I thought I had it memorized, I would forget a line on one day or a word on another day. In the meantime, Greek Independence Day was rapidly approaching, along with my increasing anxiety. One mistake and we faced the anger of the teacher as well as the priest, bringing embarrassment to our families. It became my worst nightmare. I was overcome with anxiety and nausea as I reluctantly staggered up the narrow stairway to the stage in an oversized tsarouhia, wearing a foustanella and carrying a rifle, to stand before the Greek community to recite the poem.

There I stood, in front of everyone—my proud parents, the priest, and the Greek community—trying desperately to remember the lines of the poem that I had committed to memory, which, because of anxiety, appeared to have vanished from my brain. When I think about that time, I don't remember reciting that poem or if I made any mistakes. And worse, those of our friends who didn't have to participate that year were in the audience laughing at us dressed in our authentic outfits as we struggled through our verses.

Because of my Greekness, I continue to celebrate Greek Independence Day by waking up to sing the Greek National Anthem, to the amusement of my wife, followed by making a telephone call and playing a recording of the Greek National Anthem to my daughter, who has learned to expect it every year. Rather than a shirt and tie, I wear a Greek soccer shirt to the clinic, which is always an interesting topic of conversation. And, of course, if the schedule permits, rather than marching down Vasilissis Sophias Avenue in formation into Syntagma to guard the Tomb of the Unknown Soldier, I settle for a trip to the Hellenic Cultural Center in the evening to meet with my fellow evzones. Yassou! "Long live Greece!" (Ζητω Ελλας!)

Having dropped me off at the Greek school, my father usually went to the coffeehouse across from Kalivas Park to play cards, and I would walk there to meet him when Greek school concluded for the day.

Entering the coffeehouse required a forceful push against the heavy, brown weathered wood door that seemed to be jammed on its rusty hinges. Once inside, my olfactory bulbs would immediately become aroused by the combined smell of cigar and cigarette smoke that made the air heavy and musty. I wondered if the windows were ever opened or if they even could be opened. At the same time, I was confronted by an old, unpolished, dented, brass spittoon on the floor to the left with cigar and cigarette butts strewn on the floor near it. They must have been near misses attributed to the poorly lit room.

As I proceeded warily into the interior, a few dim light bulbs hanging from the low, smoke-stained metal ceiling barely cast enough light to see any detail with clarity. A church calendar hanging from one of the posts that supported the metal ceiling and old weathered tables on either side of the room eventually became apparent. Some were occupied by men smoking, playing cards, and drinking coffee.

At other tables, men appeared to be reading Greek newspapers, despite the scarcity of light, although I don't know how that was possible. I was startled by the condition of the wooden floor—old, undulating, uneven, creaky, unpolished, and dirt stained, giving me the feeling that it could collapse under me at any moment.

The poorly maintained state of the floor was representative of many of the structures within the Greek section of the city and typified the neglect they endured during that period. As I surveyed the smoke-filled room, my eyes suddenly locked in on an old man sitting alone at a table close to the window with an expressionless face and a vacant stare. His countenance was a compelling sign of his apparent loneliness and was accentuated by the hollowness in his eyes that seemed to lack focus while he slowly twirled his komboloi, a string of Greek worry beads. Perhaps he was thinking of an earlier, happier time in Greece or of his family and how much he loved them or the loneliness that he presently endured.

For some undetermined reason, detaching my gaze from that old man became especially difficult. The reason would become apparent but not until many years later. It is fascinating how the brain functions, because the image of that old man sitting alone at that table by the window continues to persist in my subconscious memory and can be activated instantaneously by an explicit thought or event.

In the rear, next to a small, makeshift kitchen area that included a small refrigerator and a cast-iron wood-fired cooking stove, stood an old pot-bellied stove that supplied marginal heat to the dank interior during the winter. During this period, I can remember that the men hunched over and kept their overcoats on while playing cards.

Finally, in that ethereal space, I spotted my father with his hat tipped back, exposing his forehead, wearing his woolen sport coat with bowtie still fastened, totally immersed in a card game with one of his friends. As I approached him, the coffeehouse attendant graciously offered me a soda and a piece of baklava, a Greek pastry—a custom that is impolite to refuse. I will never forget any detail about that coffeehouse, and I will always remember the impressions and images of a unique place that provided happiness and camaraderie for those Greek men. Further, that place reminds me of an earlier time, of my father, and of those less complicated days that existed during my childhood. Whenever I think of them, I become nostalgic.

Glendi

During the summer months, the Greek church sponsors several regularly scheduled Sunday outings, called glendi, that begin in the afternoon and continue into the evening. Held on Church-owned property in a country location not far from the city to make it accessible for as many people as possible to attend, glendi are festive events, where Greek families congregate to escape the summer heat, to meet with friends, to eat and dance, and perhaps to have an occasional alcoholic beverage. Glendi provide a physical and expressive occasion that supports the Greek culture and its heritage, and they were regular family events for us. These *Sunday Greek picnic days*, as we called them, were times when Greek families could congregate and enjoy some of the cultural traditions together. Children could play together while their parents could dance to the sounds of the bouzouki and the clarinet. They represented a time when families could withdraw from the assimilation of the workweek and experience a sense of Greekness.

As soon as we arrived in the midafternoon and parked our 1955 Chevrolet in a large, unpaved field adjacent to the picnic area, I could hear the mesmerizing sounds of the bouzouki and clarinet. At the same time, the aroma of tender lamb being roasted on an open fire pit acted as an attractant and guided us toward the entrance, the scent becoming stronger and more inviting as we approached. The picnic area was sheltered within a grove of white pines at the base of a hill and consisted of several weathered buildings of various sizes that surrounded a cement dance floor and a nearby gazebo for the orchestra.

To the left of the picnic area entrance stood the main building, a conspicuously large, long, one-story, green, weathered wooden structure with a pinecone-laden roof. It had several large open, frameless windows along both its sides with wooden shutters that could be closed during inclement weather but that otherwise remained open to allow the fresh, pine-scented air to drift through and promote a sense of relaxation.

A basic kitchen was positioned at one end, where participants could purchase spanakopita, lamb dinners, and pastries. Within the kitchen were several rows of worn wooden tables and benches, where people could sit, eat, drink, and relax. Left of the main building stood a smaller, weather-beaten, brown, wooden, shed-like structure sheltered between two large pine trees. It was placed strategically close to the cement dance floor and housed liquor available for purchase. Wine, beer, ouzo, and home-brewed liquor was followed by an energetic toast to our health and then, in Zorba-like fashion, the dance!

Behind these two buildings was an area enclosed by cement blocks that created a large fire pit used for roasting lamb. I can still visualize the men working the fire pit—red faced from the fire, or from the liquor, or perhaps from both—standing authoritatively over the lamb in their long aprons and turning the spits.

Approximately twenty yards in front of the main building was the heart of the picnic area—a large, circular, cement dance floor set under a grove of sheltering white pines surrounded by rows of weather-beaten and splintered wooden tables and benches. Strung between the pines above the dance floor, several light bulbs delivered marginal light but added a certain aesthetic attraction. I remember that they frolicked and twinkled merrily as they darted and hid behind the pines when the wind blew. Adjacent to the dance floor, a large, white gazebo accommodated a local Greek orchestra that played music from various regions of Greece, almost without interruption throughout the afternoon and evening.

Although the orchestra played songs from various regions of Greece, most of the Greeks in this community were from the Macedonian region, so music and dance from this region, the tsamiko, predominated. As the afternoon progressed, and encouraged by more ouzo and tsipouro, the dancing became more expressive. Men danced dressed in black pants, white dress shirts with sleeves rolled up above the elbows, collars unbuttoned exposing gold crosses extending from chains that seemed to reach for the heavens, with their arms extended as if beseeching the gods for renewed energy. Clearly, they were thoroughly enjoying themselves, as exemplified by the mesmerized expressions on their faces.

Boundaries

Growing up as Greek Americans, certain elements were so deeply ingrained into our heads by our parents and relatives that, when we confronted any one of them, we automatically withdrew without hesitation and did not dare to transgress. Let me share with you some examples of taboos enforced by both our parents and members of our extended family as well.

For one, we were cautioned never to drink from other people's glasses or bottles or share their utensils when eating, because it was unsanitary. However, it mystified me that the entire church congregation could receive Holy Communion from the same spoon, but my mother never seemed to worry about that. Also, many of my Greek friends and I were prohibited from swimming in public pools, because they might have been unsanitary. Furthermore, there was the fear that we would drown! No wonder none of us learned how to swim as children.

When Louie turned seventeen, he obtained his driver's license, and that evening he proudly picked me up in his father's new, shiny, royal blue Buick Roadmaster hardtop convertible, and we drove to an outdoor hot dog stand where most of the kids our age hung out. I was fifteen and was sternly directed by my mother to be back home by 9:00 p.m.

While we were there, one of Louie's friends repeatedly dared him to a race on the adjacent highway, and Louie finally capitulated and foolishly accepted the challenge. George, Chris, and I rode in the car, terrified, while the two cars were hurtling down the highway neck and neck. Louie shifted the automatic transmission into low gear to generate more power. It was a successful maneuver and, despite the black smoke that continuously emitted from the exhaust, we forged ahead and won the race.

Regrettably, as we learned later, our victory was at the expense of the car's transmission. Further, as fate would have it, at approximately 8:15, as we were loading up the car to come home, it would not start. In a desperate attempt to meet my curfew, I panicked and began to walk (run!) home. The problem was that I lived at least four miles from the hot dog stand, and there was no way I was going to make it by 9:00 p.m. As the compassionate gods would have it, Louie finally got the car started and picked me up along the route, and I barely made it in time. That was a night that I will never forget!

The GAGMS and Dating

The Greeks take credit for establishing a positioning system that I call the Greek Awareness and Global Monitoring System (GAGMS), possibly a forerunner to GPS, and Gus Portokalos from *My Big Fat Greek Wedding* will undoubtedly insist that GPS evolved from the GAGMS as well. This was an elaborate system that had an uncanny ability to swiftly provide critical information to parents regarding the location of their children, as well as who they were with. We eventually became aware of this system, but being helpless to disengage it, we ultimately accepted it as part of our lives in the Greek section.

When I was sixteen years old, my parents eased their restrictions somewhat, and I was permitted to leave the house periodically in the early evenings with the condition that they knew who I was going to be with and, of course, that girls were excluded. My friends and I would usually meet at Aurore's restaurant across the street from the Sacred Heart Hospital on Hanover Street, a popular spot as well for student nurses who lived in the adjacent residence across from the hospital.

Despite any interest that may have developed, we rarely engaged in any conversation with the nurses, because Aurore's was owned and operated by Greeks, and if Greeks saw you talking to the nursing students, the GAGMS would be quickly activated, and your parents would know before you got home. But the GAGMS was much more extensive than that, and its tentacles seemed to reach everywhere.

Three doors down on the same side of the street as the restaurant was an Italian sandwich shop owned and operated by Chris, a silver-haired distinguished Greek gentleman, who stood behind the counter ready to satisfy your gastronomic needs. But he was prepared to do more than that. On the wall behind the counter, within easy reach, was a telephone, and any attempt to arrange a clandestine meeting with a student nurse or any young lady in his shop would prompt him to put on his thick, black, horn-rimmed glasses and quickly telephone our parents.

And, as many of you remember, regardless of our efforts to avoid detection, the GAGMS was all-encompassing, extending beyond the Greek section, and it functioned flawlessly! Occasionally, with our parents' approval, my friends and I would routinely meet in the early evening at the Red Arrow Diner located on the Daniel Webster Highway or at the Merrimack Fruit in downtown Manchester to talk about sports and other topics of interest to high school boys. And, of course, these establishments were owned and operated by Greeks, and our behavior was constantly monitored there as well.

Further, on Thursday nights, the shops in Manchester would remain open until 9:00 p.m., and with our parents' approval, we would meet at the Puritan Restaurant on Elm Street, which was owned by Greeks as well, and that meant continued scrutiny by the GAGMS. Any form of behavior that simulated misconduct, even though it may have been misinterpreted as such, meant a telephone call to our parents and a loss of the few privileges that we enjoyed.

One further comment regarding the GAGMS: The chief of police in Manchester was also a Greek! Without a doubt, growing up as a Greek American in the 1950s in the Greek section was quite an experience, and although I never considered it unusual, it probably was because I didn't know any better. Now, however, when I think about those times and our naivety, I simply shake my head and smile broadly.

Let's proceed to a more byzantine issue as far as Greeks are concerned—dating! Does this word even exist among Greeks? Of course! They have assumed credit for most words and phrases, and for dating, it is τακτοπιοημενο γαμο, *arranged marriage*. An arranged marriage or matchmaking (προξηνιαδες), once an important tradition among the Greeks, fortunately has become less significant in contemporary Greek society. The following is an example of how it works and the chaos that is likely to develop once it is initiated.

I was visiting my aunt Effie with my mother one night when she excitedly advised us that her son Georgie was going to become married. Her mother-in-law, my aunt Migthalou, arranged with her friends in Greece for their daughter to come to America to marry her grandson Georgie. Georgie was seventeen years old, frail, shy, introverted, and did not speak Greek. Furthermore, the girl from Greece and her mother had arrived in Manchester and would be here at any minute. So much for a dull, routine visit with the relatives. I couldn't wait to see this Greek tragedy unfold.

When the girl arrived with her mother, I knew immediately that any prospect of marriage was doomed. The young lady was lively, attractive, but unfortunately for poor Georgie, she spoke primarily Greek. This was marriage arrangement (προξηνιαδες) at its finest. Not wanting to interfere with a developing romance, I said good night and left.

According to my mother, who assumed the role of the village reporter, the chosen couple sat and stared at each other for hours at a time, and this agonizing courtship persevered for several days with all communication between them requiring interpretation by my aunt, Georgie's grandmother. And her interpreting skills remained questionable. Finally, the young lady's level of maturity, intuition, and good Greek sense, facilitated by their inability to communicate, resulted in her premature departure and a rapid return to Greece. Obviously, Georgie and his family were devastated and couldn't understand why she had left, but obviously the arrangement was doomed from the outset. This was dating the Greek way.

Other than the preceding example, if you were brought up as a Greek American in my generation, you were prohibited from dating, and that issue was not debatable. Moreover, events such as school dances and proms were forbidden as well. I remember that the junior prom was scheduled for May 4, the evening following a high school baseball game. To allow the juniors on the team to attend the prom, the game started earlier that afternoon. However, that was of no significance to me or the other two Greek junior ballplayers on the team. The closest we were going to get to the prom would be to place corsages on each other's wrists.

For Greek Americans of my generation, a prerequisite to dating was a formal engagement blessed by the local priest. Prior to that, the Greek interpretation of dating was sitting in the parlor with a Greek young lady in the presence of one or more of her family members and *only* if the father approved of the *Greek* young man. Getting the Greek young lady out of the house required a formal engagement. And you notice that I use the term *Greek* young lady, because dating a non-Greek young lady was prohibited in those days and, in many instances, continues to be strongly discouraged.

Not only was dating forbidden, but any discussion of sex was forbidden in the Greek community as well, at least for me and my close friends, and any transgression would have easily been detected by the GAGMS.

I think that this naivety was typical of our generation in a more global sense as well, however, and not confined merely to the Greeks. We had no formal sex education, and our ignorance regarding this subject can be illustrated by a rather amusing and authentic account regarding self-taught sex education that we received informally while in high school. A group of us were in my father's car one evening (beyond detection by the GAGMS), and my friend Chris was in the back seat with a young Greek girl named Aphrodite, who was sitting on his lap. Later, having dropped her off at her home, we went to the Red Arrow Diner to have a coffee, and we noticed that Chris was clearly distressed. Following an extensive interrogation, he finally admitted that he was concerned that Aphrodite might be pregnant.

Shocked by that possibility, we pursued the issue further and asked him why he thought she might be pregnant. He replied, "Because she was sitting on my lap!" Given our ignorance of anatomy, sex, and reproduction, none of us could provide an answer, but we had another Greek friend, Tom, who we regarded as an expert on most subjects and who, we were sure, could give us a definitive answer to this dilemma. We promptly called him and nervously described the details of the event, to which he asked, "Were they holding hands?" Chris replied emphatically, "No, we were not holding hands, but she was sitting on my lap." Tom replied in a confident and reassuring voice, "Well, then, there's absolutely no reason to be concerned. Since you weren't holding her hand, she is not pregnant!" We all breathed a great sigh of relief.

Marriage

In contemporary Greek society, one tradition that has not changed is that marriage is considered the normal result of adulthood. In earlier Greek society, it was considered unusual for a girl not to marry, and if she were not married, she was discouraged from living away from home. Although this attitude has diminished greatly in contemporary Greek society, it is still adhered to by older Greeks. In my generation, a young person, whether male or female, generally lived with their family until they became married, but this, too, has changed in contemporary society.

Those of you who are not Greek and have started dating a Greek most likely have quickly noticed that there are differences between the two of you as far as the Greek parents are concerned. And if you have seen *My Big Fat Greek Wedding*, your conclusion has been solidified. To a Greek, you are perceived as different, a ξενος, a foreigner, a stranger, an outsider, and one who is looked at with suspicion by the family. It should become quickly obvious that dating a Greek can be extremely difficult, because you are dating the family as well. To the Greeks, family is extremely important, and you will meet them very soon. And prepare yourself for how large and inclusive Greek families are. Do not be surprised when you arrive at their home and are confronted by twenty or thirty family members who have been hastily summoned to examine and interrogate you regarding your intentions and your life's goals. This is one of the many reasons why many non-Greeks think Greeks come from a different world.

Without question, many older Greeks continue to suffer from xenophobia and have an intense distrust for anyone who is not Greek. The following is another dilemma that non-Greeks may confront when they are dating a Greek person. Not only do Greeks mistrust non-Greeks, but they are quite likely to mistrust Greek non-family members as well. This being the case, what chance as a non-Greek do you have? It's a virtual nightmare. In some cases, family members will ignore you, and if they look at you at all, it is with suspicion, and many of them may continue to ignore you. Moreover, if a young Greek woman or man remains resolute regarding their non-Greek friend, a Greek father may look at him or her and finally, with a capitulating gesture, declare, "Well at least he or she looks like a Greek!"

This myopic cultural mindset was typical within Greek American families of my generation, and I can validate it from a personal experience. I met my wife, Pam, who is of Italian-Polish descent, while we were students at Boston University. When my parents met her for the first time, my father turned to my mother and said, "Well, Mary, she looks like a Greek." Incredible, isn't it? This is how the Greek family appears to an outsider, to a non-Greek. What else could a non-Greek think but that these people are crazy?

Despite this hysteria, Pam, who is also my best friend and tolerates my chaos, enthusiastically supports my Greekness and encourages me to retain all aspects of Hellenism. She has been the catalyst in inspiring me to write this book about Greeks and remains my steadfast supporter as I struggle to complete it. In this regard, if only my father could have lived long enough to have seen my daughter, Samantha, he would have called her his Greek goddess. A father could never ask for a more wonderful daughter. And one day, she brought home Peter, whom she met in college and who is of Italian descent. A perfect example of cultural assimilation. As I have told them, if I had to select a husband for her, I could not have done better.

A young Greek will ask the blessing of his parents in marriage, and it remains customary for him to ask the young lady's father for permission to marry as well. I asked my wife's father for permission to marry his daughter and was relieved when he gave me his approval. My son-in-law asked for my permission to marry my daughter. This is hard enough for a young Greek man, but can you imagine what it is like for a non-Greek young man asking a Greek father for permission to marry his daughter? As Alexis Zorba would say, "The full catastrophe!"

My cousin Faye was dating a young Greek man named Nick, who was studying to become an engineer, and they decided that, following graduation from college, they would marry. I left out one critical detail in this otherwise blissful tale, and most likely, many of you have already identified the missing element. It was "Dad," Faye's father, my uncle John! Like many Greek fathers, he was unaware or at least refused to believe that "his daughter" was dating! Furthermore, the prospect of his daughter's marriage was unimaginable to him, even though Nick's family was well respected within the Greek community and had come from the same region in Northern Greece as my uncle John.

Nevertheless, displaying the courage of a lioness, one evening Faye anxiously approached her father to ask his permission to marry Nick and to discuss their wedding plans. That appeared to be a perfectly reasonable request, and given the circumstances, the logical conclusion was that he would be ecstatic at the proposition. A young lady marrying a young man with the potential to be successful? What more could any father ask for? But this is a Greek father from the "old country!" As soon as he heard the word marriage, he became infuriated and went into an uncontrollable rage. It was as if her request was made to Lyssa, the Greek goddess of rage. Despite Faye's passionate appeals, her father remained steadfast in his refusal. You would expect that, given the love for his daughter, his refusal would have eventually moderated, and he would become more rational, but not in this instance. As far as he was concerned, marriage remained out of the question.

Nonetheless, despite his unrelenting attitude, my cousin, persistent in her desire to marry Nick, remained determined. Moreover, despite repeated efforts by my aunt and relatives to convince him that Nick was a fine young man worthy of marrying his daughter, he would rage whenever the discussion was initiated. Finally, when they realized that their efforts to change his mind were fruitless, and it became obvious that he was not going to capitulate, the wedding plans proceeded covertly. I was at college in Boston during this tumultuous period when I received a frantic telephone call from my mother to inform me of the volatile situation. The energy from the clandestine plot was quickly being built up within the caldera, and it was conceivable that a violent eruption could occur at any time. Chaos! But after all, we are Greeks, aren't we?

Miraculously, the wedding plans apparently proceeded without interruption, at least as far as we knew, without her father's knowledge, which was remarkable. But not without some strategic changes. On their wedding day, my cousin and her attendants excitedly, but apprehensively, dressed at our home while I stood as a sentry at the driveway entrance, unsure whether I would be attending a wedding or a funeral. I remember that day as if it were yesterday.

Traditionally, Greek weddings occur on Sundays, and unless circumstances dictated otherwise, my aunt and her daughters would be at home, but on this day, my uncle was alone. It remains inconceivable that he would sit there the entire day and not suspect that something was unusual. Could his tomato plants have occupied that much of his time and created such a diversion? Or perhaps subliminally he suspected that a plan was evolving and, despite his volatile nature and his inability to stop it, finally resigned himself to that fact? Despite our excitement, we all remained worried that my uncle John would discover the plan and attempt to disrupt the wedding.

Nevertheless, there we were, satirizing secret operatives, preparing to proceed in a clandestine operation, dressed in our formal attire, standing exposed and unprotected in the driveway, under the cover of bright sunlight, with limousines lined up to deliver us to the church. Being accustomed with a Greek's inability to keep a secret and vulnerability to the GAGMS, it was remarkable that the plan was executed without a flaw and we proceeded to the church without incident. The wedding transpired without her father's knowledge, at least as far as we knew, and my cousin was given in marriage by my uncle Al. Now the family's attention shifted toward managing the inevitability of what would occur when my uncle discovered that his daughter was married.

Following the wedding reception, when my aunt Ourania and my cousin Johanna eventually arrived home, my uncle John asked them where they had been and why Faye wasn't with them. I'm sure it wasn't easy for her, but my aunt finally admitted that Faye and Nick had been married earlier that afternoon and that they had departed on their honeymoon. The expectation was that he would explode at the news, but remarkably, rather than the expected rage, he quietly slumped back into his chair without saying a word and remained silent and disconsolate.

Eventually, when the newlyweds returned from their honeymoon, and obviously apprehensive about their reception, my uncle greeted them with such enthusiasm and passion that you would have thought he had given them his blessing from the outset. Sadly, and most regrettably, a cherished event in his daughter's life had occurred despite his protestations and in his absence. Because of his obstinacy, he had missed the marvelous opportunity to give his daughter away at her wedding. Furthermore, to our amazement, as if he had been struck by a lightning bolt from Zeus resulting in an attitude adjustment, and continuing until my uncle's death, he and Nick remained best friends, and no one could compare to his engineer son-in-law.

GROWING UP GREEK MAY APPEAR to have been very challenging, but it wasn't. We didn't know any other way. Of course, some of our non-Greek friends enjoyed greater freedom with fewer restrictions, and others had greater financial resources that afforded them more flexibility, but none of those issues seemed to bother us. We were blessed with extended families that loved us and provided as best they could for us. And, of course, we complained about having to attend Greek school, but in retrospect, what a wonderful opportunity that gave us. We developed an ability to read and write the primary language that we spoke. Despite the dissolution of the agoras as we remember them, many of us have continued to find agoras where we can congregate and maintain our Greekness.

PART III

Culture and Tradition

CHAPTER 7

The Greek Diet

"Greeks put their soul into the pot"

GREEK FOOD DIFFERS FROM REGION to region. Some foods, however, are common to all regions. Some are compatible with the Mediterranean diet, whereas others are not considered to be beneficial to cardiovascular health. I have included some of the basic Greek foods that I grew up eating.

The Mediterranean Diet

Diet, diet, diet! So many diets! How many diets have there been, how many are there now, and how many will there be in the future? Low fat, high fat, low carbohydrate, high carbohydrate, low protein, high protein, eat nothing diet, eat everything diet! Unfortunately, regardless of the claims and assurances of these diets, obesity and cardiovascular disease continue to remain global problems, and in some countries, appear to be increasing at an alarming rate. This being the unfortunate reality, the diet that has endured for many decades without receiving suitable promotion until recently is one of the most wholesome diets.

It is the Mediterranean diet, once known as the "diet of the poor," based on the dietary traditions of Crete, Greece, and southern Italy.

The rates of chronic disease within these populations are among the lowest, and life expectancy remains among the highest of any other region in the world. The Mediterranean diet consists of fish, fruits, vegetables, legumes, nuts, olive oil instead of butter, herbs and spices instead of salt, yogurt, water, and wine, of course, with minimal red meat and sweets. These elements, combined with physical activity, remain the essential ingredients for promoting good cardiovascular health and longevity and for reducing the risk of cardiovascular disease and muscle weakness. The Mediterranean diet ensures a sufficient intake of dietary antioxidants; enhances protection against cardiovascular disease, stress, and inflammation; and has also been linked to a higher brain volume. Moreover, low levels of dietary antioxidants are associated with loss of muscle mass (sarcopenia) and strength, leading to compromised physical function.[3]

As an example of the beneficial effects of the Mediterranean diet, the population on the island of Ikaria in the Mediterranean has been documented as one of the healthiest and longest living populations in the world. Men on Ikaria are four times as likely as American men to reach the age of ninety.[4,5] It has been given the distinction as the island where people forget to die. That Americans have a lower longevity, given our technology, resources, and knowledge regarding healthy lifestyles, is unacceptable.

In the olive oil–rich Mediterranean diet, not all fats are considered unhealthy. Even though total fat content may comprise more than 40 percent

---

3   Mayo Clinic Staff, "Mediterranean Diet: A Heart-Healthy Eating Plan," Mayo Clinic, accessed July 26, 2018, https://www.mayoclinic.org/healthy-lifestyle/nutrition-and-healthy-eating/in-depth/mediterranean-diet/art-20047801.

4   Dan Buettner, "The Island Where People Forget to Die," *The New York Times Magazine*, October 24, 2012, https://www.nytimes.com/2012/10/28/magazine/the-island-where-people-forget-to-die.html.

5   Diane Kochilas, "Ikaria: The Mindful Mediterranean Diet on the Greek Island Where People Forget to Die," HuffPost, December 2, 2014, https://www.huffingtonpost.com/diane-kochilas/ikaria-the-mindful-medite_b_5920490.html.

of the traditional diet, it is primarily in the form of good fat, or monounsaturated fat, primarily from olive oil, which produces fewer tissue-destructing free radicals and has been shown to have a significant protective effect against cardiovascular disease.

OLIVES AND OLIVE OIL

Daily Greek dishes include meals cooked with olive oil and soups and salads rich in olive oil. Historically, the significance of olive oil goes back to Athena, the goddess of wisdom. According to mythology, she and Poseidon, the god of the sea, were in a competition to name the city of Athens, and when Athena thrust her staff into the ground, an olive tree suddenly emerged. She won the competition, and the city was named for her. The olive branch remains a symbol of peace, and the olive wreath is symbolic of Olympic victory.

"Olives, olive oil, and lemon. Everything you eat seems to have olive oil and lemon on it!" "How do you get everything to taste so good?" I heard these comments while having dinner at a Greek restaurant recently and smiled. A persuasive argument can be made that the most important Greek food is the olive! And why not, since Greece is the third leading producer of olives. Therefore, olive oil must be considered an essential staple of Greek culture. Olive oil is always present in the Greek home, whether on a Greek table, where it is used as a salad dressing, or for bread dipping, or stored in the pantry until it can be utilized for cooking.

FISH

Fish, rather than meat, has always been an integral part of the Mediterranean diet. The evidence is compelling regarding fish consumption and its role in the prevention of coronary artery disease because of the cardiovascular benefits of omega-3 fatty acids. Fish is especially popular if your family came from one of the Greek islands or a mainland shore village. Even though my parents came from the mountains, they constantly reminded me that if I wanted to be smart, I had to eat fish. Without a doubt, I should have listened more closely to my parents and eaten more fish.

Whenever I bring non-Greek friends to a Greek restaurant for an authentic dinner, they often ask me to recommend specific items for their meal. If they prefer fish, I usually recommend the porgy (τσιπουρα), a fatty white fish with a mild flavor and firm flakes (high in omega-3 fatty acids and low in calories, also known as the Royal Dorado in many upscale Greek restaurants). It is a tasty, bony white fish that is generally basted in a mixture of olive oil and lemon juice and pan fried or grilled. In most Greek restaurants, it is generally presented filleted and garnished appropriately. It may also be presented intact with the waiter skillfully filleting it at the table.

When I ordered the Royal Dorado for dinner one evening at the Grand Resort in Lagonissi, Greece, in the Saronic Gulf not far from Athens, the waiter, displaying the skill of a surgeon, filleted the fish effortlessly with a spoon. Don't expect to see the porgy filleted and presented this way at the Hartford Hellenic Cultural Center, however. Instead, the porgy is generally presented intact with its head and tail hanging limply over the edges of an undersized plate complemented by a mound of greens (χορτα), garnished with a lemon cut in half. If the person dining is not Greek and is unaccustomed to this presentation, the typical response is confusion, followed by a nervous laugh, a brief period of silence, and finally an appeal to me as to, "What should I do now?" I calmly respond, "Now you eat it." Nevertheless, not allowing the diner to agonize any further, and especially if she is a lady and remains squeamish, the fish is usually returned to the kitchen and quickly reappears filleted. Otherwise, a brief course in dissection by one of the Greek diners at the table generally results in effective bone removal.

Last, but most important, are the instructions on the "Greek method" of eating this fish, by using the fingers. Incidentally, the lemon wedge, in addition to enhancing the flavor, is especially useful for cleaning the hands and removing the fish odor.

DAIRY

Although the intake of dairy products is generally low among Greeks, the consumption of low-fat feta cheese and yogurt is high. Perhaps no food has made such a successful impact in the name of health than the currently available Greek-style yogurt. Even though, in some cases, it may not be authentic Greek yogurt, the label identifies it as such, and as Mr. Portokalos would say, "Yogurt is a Greek word!"

The creamy, multiflavored "Greek-style" yogurt with fruit and nuts that is exceptionally popular and currently available in many grocery stores, specialty shops, and health food stores bears little resemblance to the yogurt I grew up with. The only yogurt available to us as children consisted of a thick, amorphous, white, lumpy, unflavored, brackish-tasting yogurt that was generally homemade and poured into an unmarked, sealed quart preservative bottle. Infrequently, it was available at a Greek grocery store.

In those days, yogurt was consumed almost exclusively in Greek and other Mediterranean cultures. But then again, who else would subject themselves to such a brackish delight? As a child, homemade yogurt was always available in the refrigerator, and whenever I was hungry, that's what I would eat as a snack. And given Greek originality, it could have been mixed with honey, fruit, or cucumbers. Without understanding the beneficial effects of the bacterial flora in yogurt, it was the homeopathic remedy of choice whenever I had a sore throat or a stomachache as a child. In addition to the health benefits of yogurt, it is currently used as a cosmetic, as a beauty mask, and as a remedy for sunburned skin, as well as for stomach disorders.

APPETIZERS

Whenever eating at a Greek restaurant or even at home, appetizers (μεζεδακια, ορετικα) are generally served prior to a main dish. Nevertheless, be wary if you are unfamiliar with them, because even though delicious, they are only a prelude of what is to come, so reserve some space for the main course. On many occasions, appetizers may be eaten as the main dish accompanied by bread and wine. Among the popular appetizers (mezethakia, oretika) are cheese, radishes, almonds, figs, anchovies, olives, stuffed grape leaves, octopus, squid, and bread with olive oil or hummus. These are followed by a main course that may include either fish or meat and ends with yogurt, fruit, and honey—perhaps a throwback to the gods' love of ambrosia and nectar followed by a cup of demitasse coffee. Depending on the circumstances and the requirements of the following day, ouzo, an anise-flavored spirit distilled from grapes, might be served to conclude the evening and/or in some instances, to extend it. Opa!

Having been forewarned of this Greek dining custom, I will cite an example that occurred recently while my colleague and I were at a conference at the Grand Resort in Lagonissi, Greece. A reception followed by dinner was held one evening for the conference participants. The reception was held in a large outdoor terrace and adjoining balcony that provided a majestic view of the peninsula and the bay. It continued for approximately two hours and included several types of hors d'oeuvres that not only satisfied the most critical gastronomic palate but that could have easily qualified as dinner. When the reception ended, a series of large, floor-to-ceiling collapsible separating doors were opened, revealing a most elegant banquet area with spectacular views of the Saronic Gulf. Dinner was served!

Less elegant but equally healthy, typical meals at the Hartford Hellenic Cultural Center generally follow the Mediterranean diet, although other less healthy items are also served upon request. No menus are available, but Alekos, the octogenarian chef, waiter, and dishwasher, will eagerly escort you into his undersized kitchen and display his entrées. For the first plate, Alekos will serve an appetizer consisting of anchovies, giant beans, olives, roasted peppers, feta cheese, Greek bread, and olive oil, followed by a peasant, χωριατικι, or village salad that includes tomatoes, cucumbers, onions, feta cheese, and Kalamata olives garnished with oregano and immersed in extra virgin olive oil. Incidentally, any excess olive oil on the plate is usually absorbed by the Greek bread.

MAIN COURSE

For the main plate, selections usually include any of the following items: from the sea, porgy, traditionally served with lemon slices and greens, or squid and octopus, caught locally and cooked daily; from the land, steak (μπριζολα), marinated in extra virgin olive oil and garlic and served with thinly cut pan-fried (in extra virgin olive oil) potatoes, or skewered pork in a pita bread wrap.

Red wine or beer generally fortifies the spirit for the defense at Thermopylae. Nevertheless, while attaining kefi, Greeks frown on excess alcohol consumption. Low to moderate consumption of alcohol has been associated with an increase in HDL (good cholesterol) levels and a reduction in the risk of developing coronary artery disease (CAD). These positive results have been attributed to alcohol's relaxative effect on blood vessels, as well as antiplatelet effects similar to aspirin.

The last plate is likely to consist of Greek yogurt—plain or with honey or fruit—or a plate of mixed fruit. For those with nocturnal aspirations, a cup of demitasse coffee followed by a sleepless night, or a shot of ouzo (τσιμπορο) or the traditional "γεια σου" and a peaceful night's sleep, might be prescribed.

By the way, if porgy is your choice, don't be offended if Nikos, the club's most sociable member and local Hellenic ambassador, approaches you and declares, "Oh, you can't be Greek, because you are using utensils to eat the fish. We use our fingers!" Greeks have an amazing ability to pick the porgy clean with their fingers, no offense, of course, to Emily Post. Also, the porgy is served with the head and tail intact, so be sure it doesn't wink at you!

DANDELIONS

I still look forward to boiled dandelions smothered in extra virgin olive oil and lemon, and they are always available at the local Hellenic Cultural Center. I have introduced them to my non-Greek friends, and they look forward to them as well.

How important are dandelions to the Greeks? As many of you know, dandelions, in addition to their nutritive value, are an important food source for the Greeks. Furthermore, their collection is an extraordinary social event that is worth noting. Dandelions. Let's go to the reservoir and pick dandelions (Ας παμε στη δεξαμενη και διαλεξετε πικλαριδες).

If you are a Greek, you know what dandelion greens are. Without question, picking dandelions has always been and continues to be an important nutritive as well as social event for Greeks. Nutritionally, they are rich in iron and are abundantly available in the local fields, making them easily accessible to most Grecian pickers.

Without a doubt, because of their extensive knowledge about most things, Greek grandmothers know everything, and choosing the most appropriate time for picking dandelions is no exception. Inspired by what they apparently perceive to be a cool, refreshing Aegean breeze but instead is a hot, stifling summer wind with the temperature in the nineties and the sun at its zenith, Greek grandmothers will embark on their adventure into the reservoir to pick dandelions.

I remember several occasions when I would be sitting under the protective shade of the grape trellis at home on a hot, humid summer afternoon, and suddenly the call to action would sound, and the assault team, as well as the support unit, was rapidly, although begrudgingly, assembled. I will never forget this image, and I am certain that many of you will find it humorous as I describe it to you. The assault unit was comprised of four overweight elderly Greek ladies, aunts, and grandmothers, who otherwise constantly complained of persistent, debilitating back, hip, and knee pain that prevented them from moving quickly. In this circumstance, however, and without hesitation, they would eagerly cram themselves into the back seat of my father's non-air-conditioned car in the sweltering heat with the windows wide open and proceed toward Derryfield Park on the outskirts of Manchester.

And this event occurred on a regular basis—four grandmothers, each one shouting instructions to my father simultaneously as to how and where to proceed. Finally, as we would drive into Derryfield Park, one of my aunts, who apparently was appointed the sentry, would suddenly identify dandelions in the field and order my father to stop.

Even before the ignition could be turned off, the car shuddered as the Greek "brigade" on their hunt for dandelions struggled to exit. Hastily pushing and shoving, one after another, they would eventually exit the vehicle and promptly survey the meadow. Suddenly, rather than springing into the countryside like a group of euphoric pixies, they would epitomize a group of penguins as they waddled into the field in their black mourning outfits, complete with heavy black stockings knotted just below the knees, jeopardizing the circulation to their lower legs. And I can't forget to mention the black scarves swathed over their heads to protect them from the sun and the black sweaters to shield them from the "breeze." And, of course, to increase traction as they proceeded into the uneven terrain, they would wear their heavy black-laced shoes with the thick heels. Greek logic at its finest, but that's the way it was.

When the dandelions were identified, they would pounce on them like a frenzied flock of giant crows. I can still visualize that scene as they would shuffle excitedly up the hill with dresses and bags blowing in the wind, knives and spatulas in their hands, preparing to descend onto their victims to collect an essential Greek delicacy.

Temporary tranquility was achieved when the bags were filled, their mission was completed successfully, and the dandelions were brought home, immediately boiled, and served that night with lemon and extra virgin olive oil, accompanied by Greek bread and homemade red wine. Admittedly, the taste of those freshly picked dandelions with lemon and oil was delicious, and the adventure, and it always was an adventure, despite the heat, was worth the effort. In those days, in addition to their nutritional value, dandelions helped sustain us during times of scarcity.

If I close my eyes, I can still visualize my aunts Mary, Harriet, and Migthalou (Θειες Μαρια, Χαρικλια, και Μιγδαλου) charging through the reservoir's meadow, despite the bright midday sunlight shining in their excited eyes, the wind gusting against their mourning dresses and empty bags, with dandelions locked in their sight. That image remains one of the most outstanding cherished memories of my youth.

SOUP

Beans are an important component of the Mediterranean diet, and two of my favorite Greek soups are fasoulatha (φασολαδα) and faki (φακη), both thick, hearty bean soups with an occasional clove of semi-sautéed garlic struggling to rise to the surface after it has released its flavor. These soups are usually eaten with a circular loaf of Greek white or wheat bread with a thick, hard crust.

As a child, I remember that several of my aunts would have to soak the bread in the soup to soften its hard crust before they could chew it and to reduce the risk of breaking their remaining teeth. These soups are substantial enough to comprise the entire meal, and believe me, once you finish them, more than likely, you are completely satisfied. Incidentally, Greeks consider bread a gift from the gods, and we would make the sign of the cross over a freshly baked loaf of bread with a knife before it was served. Also, because of its significance, we would never discard bread. If any remained after the meal was completed, it was broken up and given to animals.

As Greeks, we have all been brought up with the understanding that chicken soup was an effective treatment for a cold or respiratory condition. And in our generation, that meant homemade chicken soup. I can't count the number of times that I walked by the kitchen stove when my eyes caught a glimpse of something that suddenly popped up from the boiling caldera. And as quickly as it appeared, it submerged into the broth once again. When it surfaced again, I would notice that it was a bone with five yellow toes, complete with claws extending from them. And this was supposed to be healthy and augment the flavor?

CHESTNUTS

"Chestnuts Roasting on an Open Fire," a song made popular by Johnny Mathis and heard frequently during the winter season and Christmas, reminds us of another Greek favorite—chestnuts (καστανα). A favorite Greek item, especially in the winter, but unlike the popular song and much less romantic, you will most likely find them in a Greek home roasting on a kitchen stove burner or in the oven for twenty minutes, after which the skin peels off easily, leaving a delicious treat. The aroma of roasting chestnuts is absolutely tantalizing, and whenever I visit New York City in the winter, the smell of roasting chestnuts from the street vendor carts reminds me of those winter evenings when my mother would roast them on the kitchen burner. I can remember her telling me that they were difficult to digest, and if I ate too many at night, I might get a stomachache and would have difficulty sleeping. As always, the Greeks have a saying for everything, and, with respect to chestnuts, "to pull someone's chestnuts out of the fire" suggests boldness and bravery.

TRAHANA

When I was young, instead of the popular boxed, sugar-coated breakfast cereals available currently on supermarket shelves with a prize somewhere in their contents, I had to be satisfied with trahana (τραχανα), a cracked wheat that was soaked in milk and then home dried in the sun or purchased at the local agora. It could be either sweet or sour, depending on the milk it was soaked in. Eaten by itself, it is a wholesome and hearty food, and often served for breakfast and in the winter. Usually, my mother would prepare it with feta cheese and loukaniko (pork sausage), and primarily because of its aroma, it was difficult to eat in the morning. Even though I attempted to avoid it, admittedly, it fortified me to make the one and one-half mile trek to school on those cold, snowy winter mornings, since there were no school buses in those days. Served by itself or with feta cheese, it could be included as part of the Mediterranean diet, but with the addition of loukaniko, that becomes another issue, which we will address later.

SPANAKOPITA

And then there is spanakopita (σπανακοπιτα). How can you be a Greek and not like spanakopita? Even non-Greeks like spanakopita. Greeks from all parts of Greece love spanakopita, a pie made with spinach or leeks and feta cheese within layers of filo dough. If the filo dough is brushed lightly with butter, this dish may be included in the Mediterranean diet; otherwise, it is marginal. Spanakopita remains one of my favorite foods, and I would always ask for it whenever I visited my aunts' homes as a child. Unfortunately, my mother never acquired the ability to make it appropriately, and unlike her sisters or my aunts, her spanakopita was greasy and not flaky.

The Non-Mediterranean Diet

Greeks will reluctantly admit that not everything we eat is drawn from the "nectar of the gods," thus decreasing the likelihood that we will attain immortality. The following foods are not part of the Mediterranean diet and, if eaten on a regular basis, may be contributing factors in the promotion of peripheral vascular and coronary artery disease.

LAMB

As popular as fish is, most people know that lamb is *the* big Greek dish. Lamb is the absolute choice of meat for the holidays among the Greeks, and a must for Easter. Failure to eat it may subject you to the evil eye, and since I don't eat it, I continue to wear the evil eye.

Whenever people realize that I am a Greek and don't like lamb, they look at me funny and question my heritage. As a matter of fact, when I was dating my wife in college, and she told her mother that I was Greek, her mother exclaimed, "He's Greek? Well you better make him some lamb!" Of course, at that time neither of them was aware that I didn't like lamb and hadn't eaten it since I was forced to try it as a child. Therefore, lamb it was going to be. And even though I didn't like it, I didn't want to ruin Pam's efforts, so I braced myself to struggle through the dinner with a smile. Miraculously, on that ominous day, as the lamb was baking in the oven, it burned. Zeus, the benevolent and omnipotent almighty god, understandably recognized my distress and hurled a thunderbolt down, and I was spared. Without question, the gods were compassionate, so much so that they arranged to have a pizza delivered. My wife and I laugh about that incident frequently, and to this day, I still have not eaten any lamb. As peculiar as this seems, I recently learned that a friend of mine, a Greek restaurateur who was born on Rhodes, also doesn't eat lamb. Perhaps I'm not so strange after all.

Lamb is usually baked at home in the oven, or if the family is large or if extended family members and guests are expected, it may be baked in an oven at a Greek bakery and tenderly carried home wrapped in a large, grease-stained brown paper bag by a proud family member, usually the father who ultimately presents it to the family. Depending on the region in Greece, there are variations on how it is prepared and served, but usually it is accompanied by greens, bread, salad, feta cheese, olives, and, of course, rice pilaf. We can't forget the rice pilaf. Greeks eat rice pilaf with everything—chicken, lamb, fish, breakfast, by itself, and as a snack. And if it isn't rice pilaf, it is lemon potatoes, roasted in the oven simmering in lamb juice, chicken juice, or in a tomato sauce. Potatoes prepared this way are delicious, and I don't know a Greek, or an Italian, for that matter, or anyone else who doesn't love them. And naturally, all of this is accompanied by good Greek wine.

LOUKANIKO

What Greek doesn't like loukaniko, a pork sausage made with either leeks or oranges? Although not a part of the Mediterranean diet for obvious reasons, it is very popular and is customarily served as an appetizer, usually sliced in quarter-sized slices about one-fourth-inch thick and pan fried in its juices to maximize its flavor. When I woke up in the winter and prepared for school, I often found it floating in my trahana.

Preparing homemade loukaniko is an old art that regrettably is rapidly disappearing, primarily because its preparation is a laborious process, and it can now be purchased commercially. In addition, interest in making it is apparently fading among the younger generations. Unfortunately, the commercially made brands that I have tried cannot compare to the homemade loukaniko. As dismal as this portrayal appears, older Greeks of Macedonian heritage continue to make it, although their numbers are decreasing. Nevertheless, if you are persistent enough, and you conduct a thorough search, with good luck you may find it in selected agoras. A small agora remains in Manchester, New Hampshire that periodically has freshly made loukaniko. The proprietor knew my mother and father, and periodically I plead with him to save some for me.

Prior to driving to Manchester to visit my mother and relatives, I telephone the proprietor of the Greek agora to inquire whether he has any fresh loukaniko. His wife knows how to prepare it, and she makes it occasionally for the local Greek restaurant and for other customers as well. If he has some available, and if I can coerce him to save some for me, I put a cooler filled with ice into the trunk of my car and drive off with great anticipation, because the aroma and taste of freshly pan-fried, home-prepared loukaniko is an indescribably delightful Greek favorite.

Here, however, is where the story becomes intriguing and often disconcerting. On more than one occasion when I arrive at his agora and request twenty-five pounds of loukaniko, the proprietor becomes incredulous. Moreover, despite continuing to smile politely, he vehemently rejects my request, emphasizing that not only does he have to distribute it to the local Greek restaurant, but also that he has to save some for other customers.

However, after a lengthy discussion that includes pleading and coercion, and continually emphasizing that I drove 150 miles from Connecticut for his loukaniko, he asks me how my mother is, and I end up with twenty pounds, which I quickly pack in ice before he has a chance to reconsider. It continues to amaze him that I will travel from Connecticut to purchase fresh loukaniko, and I am sure that this is a topic of discussion at his local kafenion. Obviously, he fails to realize that a dish I was brought up with, part of daily Greek life and readily available in his Greek community, is becoming a lost art and difficult to find elsewhere. As I leave his agora, I think about my discussion with him and have the feeling that in many ways, he's better off.

Knowing that my daughter's family loves that loukaniko, once I reluctantly gave my son-in-law half of that twenty pound cache. Unfortunately, I neglected to tell him to cut it into quarter-sized pieces and pan fry it. Instead, he grilled it that evening, and his family ate dried loukaniko and thought it was delicious. When I heard that approximately two pounds had gone up in smoke on the grill, I became despondent. However, since that initial culinary catastrophe, he has been counseled regarding its proper preparation.

MEATBALLS

A Greek will always look forward to meatballs and rice pilaf in tomato sauce. Made with either lamb or beef, they are crispy golf ball–sized meatballs usually served as appetizers. What makes them so different from American meatballs is the onion, garlic, oregano, mint, cumin, and parsley that is infused into the meat. Greek meatballs can also be infused with rice served in an egg lemon sauce. The aroma of them cooking is one of the most exotic and appetizing gastronomic treats that you can expose your senses to. And they taste even better than they smell.

SWEETS

Greek spoon sweets are associated with different regions within Greece and are served to welcome guests into the home. Grapes, cherries, apricots, pears, oranges, lemons, grapefruit, tangerines, figs, and prunes are among the favorites and are either made at home or purchased from specialty shops. They are served in syrup in a small ornate glass accompanied by a spoon. My favorite is the sour cherries imported from Greece that are a delicious topping with unflavored Greek yogurt.

POOR MAN'S STEW

One of the most gruesome culinary practices that could easily be described as a gastronomic horror occurred with frightening regularity in our kitchen when I was growing up. This culinary ritual occurred whenever several of my aunts in their traditional black mourning outfits, collectively resembling a religious cult, would arrive at our home. The high priestess would be clutching a suspicious-looking wrinkled, brown soiled paper bag under her arm, guarding it securely as if she were rushing toward the goal line in a football game. Charging through the kitchen decisively, the "cult" would eventually huddle covertly in a shielded circle around a small table in the adjacent pantry. As a solitary beam of sunlight streamed into the "sanctuary" and onto the "altar," each cult member was delegated a specific duty.

One would fill a large pot with water, while another would carefully open the bag and deposit the contents inside the pot. The high priestess would then anoint the contents with seasoning as she muttered a series of inaudible mantras that resembled a mysterious religious rite. Finally, with abrupt suddenness, they would emerge, and the high priestess would place the pot on the stove burner with meticulous care as her celebrants clustered around. Although my view was partially occluded, I would be horrified by what I saw.

Within that huge pot, chunks of organ meat would bob up and down in a clear liquid surrounded by vegetables as if they were gasping for breath.

As the pot would continue to heat, steam would release, and the clear liquid would turn brownish-gray and emit an intense, wretched, rancid aroma that permeated the entire house. Horrified, I would run out the front door, thinking I must be a descendant of cannibals. Gasping for air, I couldn't imagine what could smell so putrid.

The aroma belonged to a traditional Middle Eastern dish adopted by the Greeks called *poor man's stew*, a concoction comprised of kidneys, entrails, heart, and intestines. The flavor of the organ meat is masked by vegetables and spices, such as onions, garlic cloves, salt, pepper, and paprika, to make it more palatable. The whole blend is boiled and served in a horrifying grayish-brownish–looking broth and, in my opinion, is not only a gastronomic nightmare but is likely to elevate cholesterol levels as well.

Historically, many immigrants could not afford the best cuts of meats and had to settle for organ meat as a nutritional source. Despite its apparent popularity, I have never tried it, and I don't intend to. And if that epicurean example weren't appalling enough, then the next culinary scenario was even more outlandish.

ORGAN MEAT

Occasionally, my father would arrive from the Greek bakery carrying a greasy brown paper bag under his arm while, as if on cue, several of my aunts would appear, sit at the kitchen table, and excitedly urge my father to open the bag. Without hesitation, he would proudly place the contents on a large platter, as if displaying a trophy or a centerpiece, while my aunts would stare in excitement. And what a showpiece—it would be a lamb's head.

After excitedly staring at their target and salivating for what appeared to be an eternity, they would pounce on the lamb's head, their attack resembling a group of piranhas relentlessly devouring a traditional Greek meal. *How could anyone eat this?* I would wonder.

Nonetheless, this meal is still considered a delicacy, and many Greek families continue to consume it. The historic explanation for this apparent culinary atrocity, as in the previous example, is that many earlier generations of Greek families had to settle for organ meat.

THE DIET THAT HAS BEEN practiced by Greeks and other Mediterranean people for many years, currently known as the Mediterranean diet or the heart healthy diet, has been shown to promote positive cardiovascular health. Although many foods in the Greek diet are included in the Mediterranean diet, from our preceding discussion it is obvious that some of the popular Greek foods described in this section do not promote good cardiovascular health.

In my practice, I am frequently asked this question: "I have an uncle who is ninety years old. He smokes, eats whatever he wants, still drives his automobile, and plays cards at the Greek club. How do you explain that?" My answer is: "Good genes, and the will of the gods." Research clearly indicates that adherence to most foods within the Mediterranean diet combined with a regular regimen of physical exercise is the most beneficial method of maintaining cardiovascular health. And don't forget the importance of good genes, the "will of the gods," and the "evil eye."

CHAPTER 8

Homeopathic Medicine and Superstition

"You have been smitten"

ONE OF THE MOST FASCINATING aspects of growing up Greek was the reliance on homeopathic remedies and superstitions that were practiced and utilized daily. Although many of the procedures and rituals seemed uncanny to me at that time, many, whether effective or not, continue to be utilized today.

Greek Homeopathic Medicine

My Greek aunts would put Asclepius, god of medicine in ancient Greece, to shame with their extensive knowledge of Greek homeopathic medicine. The snake-entwined staff of Asclepius remains the symbol of modern medicine. In many cases, regardless of the complaint or ailment, my aunts would most likely be consulted before a physician was because of the curative energy that flowed through their bodies and their unique ability to transfer that curative energy into the afflicted person's soma, or body.

I remember once walking into my home, shocked to see my father lying on his stomach in the parlor groaning while my aunt marched up and down his back in her stockinged feet. I laugh whenever I think of it. We had massage parlors in those days, but they were mobile, with the Greek masseuse coming to the home. Whenever my father had a backache, my aunt Migthalou, a heavy, robust woman with a silver braid knotted at the back of her head and wearing the traditional mourning outfit, would be summoned. She was one of my aunts bestowed with this miraculous curative energy. After an extensive and detailed evaluation of his condition that lasted at least thirty seconds, she would take off her heavy black shoes, and with her black stockings knotted below the knees, softly pounce on my father's back and walk assertively up and down his spine while he lay on the floor. How he survived that treatment and was able to get off the floor without several cracked ribs or vertebrae has always remained a mystery to me.

And if he didn't feel better, or if he didn't at least tell her he felt better, then she would proceed to the next protocol in her therapeutic manual, which seemed to be even more barbaric—the Greek method of cupping. This kind of therapy has become more popular as a therapeutic regimen since a modified version of cupping was used in the most recent summer Olympics. Well, without boasting, we Greeks were using that treatment for many years before it became fashionable. After carefully assembling six thick water glasses, my aunt would spit on small cotton balls and carefully insert one into each glass so the cotton ball would adhere to its base. She would then ignite the cotton ball and place each glass carefully on my father's back with meticulous precision, in accordance to a confirmed anatomical configuration.

Within a few seconds, as the oxygen became depleted, the skin under each glass would redden and expand, the result of a normal physiological response to the creation of a vacuum. However, to the young, neophyte pre-practitioner witnessing this therapeutic procedure for the first time and

HOMEOPATHIC MEDICINE AND SUPERSTITION

having no knowledge regarding the effects of a vacuum on a family member's back, observing the skin swell to the point where it appeared that it may burst at any second, surely seemed the work of the occult. Nevertheless, the skin did not rupture, and the glasses remained securely in position for approximately fifteen to twenty minutes, delivering their warranted therapeutic effects.

When the treatment had concluded, the glass cups were carefully removed from the patient's back by the skilled hands of the naturopathic physician, but, inexplicably, there would be *no change* in the patient's condition. Apart from the six red, circular, elevated welts, my father would continue to have back pain. Clearly then, the logical conclusion reached by the practitioner was that he must have been smitten by the evil eye, which required even more complex treatment. Fortunately, my aunt was an exonerator of the evil eye as well.

During those years when I was young and while my relatives continued to practice homeopathic medicine, one of my greatest fears was that my aunt would look at me and arbitrarily decide that I needed an enema, since she was endowed with the ability to examine my eyes and make that determination with certainty. Well, how bad could that be, you say? To those of you who are younger, the enemas that we were exposed to in the old days were not fleet enemas, by any means. And to those of you in my generation, I am sure you have a good idea of what I am about to describe. As you remember, the enemas in our day must have been derived from the handbook of the Marquis de Sade, and any suggestion regarding their use sent chills down our spines.

Those horrific instruments of torture consisted of a large, orange, bladder-like sack filled with warm, soapy water. The distended bladder was attached to a thin, long orange hose that had a smooth, shiny black piece of hard rubber at its end that was inserted into the appropriate target. The bladder was then suspended above the hapless victim, and utilizing the principle of gravity, once the clip was released, the warm, soapy water would surge through the narrow orange tube. The target's eyes would bulge while their intestines distended. Having been a victim of that barbaric procedure more than once, I will never forget it.

Scanning through our manual of Greek homeopathic medicine, Greeks are insistent that crushed onions have healing powers and that they can be used therapeutically as a remedy for such conditions as colds, sniffles, and bruises. Whenever I sustained an injury that resulted in a bruise, my father would quickly crush several onions with a mortar and apply a poultice to the injured area, wrapping it in a cloth bandage that remained overnight. If the Greek medicinal gods were operative, the bruise would have disappeared the next day. Incidentally, if you want my opinion on the healing powers of a crushed onion from firsthand experience, I can unequivocally say that it is ineffective. The bruise never disappeared. It would still be there the next morning. Even worse, although incredibly, nothing was said to me at school the next day, and at the time I never gave it a thought, but I can imagine what everyone at school must have been thinking—*What do these Greeks do? This kid smells like an onion!*

And, of course, who can forget the ultimate Greek panacea—olive oil! Olive oil was and remains the penultimate elixir for all maladies. In addition to its nutritive value, Greeks consider olive oil to be beneficial for digestive problems, skin irritations, coughs, and sore throats. Greeks drink olive oil for all stomach and digestive ailments, and rub it on the skin for rashes.

When I was a child, my mother made me swallow a tablespoon of olive oil every morning before going to school. I can't remember the number of times I was forced to swallow at least a tablespoon of olive oil for a stomachache. I don't recall for certain, but I don't think it ever helped. But then again, I never complained, because it was better than cod liver oil. And if I had an earache, she would pour olive oil into a tablespoon, warm it, and then, using a cotton swab, gently drop the oil into my ear.

By the way, don't underestimate the efficacy of olive oil as a potential therapeutic regimen for earaches. Recently, I directed a high school swimmer with a history of recurrent of swimmer's ear to apply two to three drops of oil into each ear before swimming as a prophylactic, because oil repels water. This is an example of a homeopathic medicine that works.

My mother would also routinely rub olive oil into my hair as a remedy for a dry scalp and to prevent dandruff. I would go to school with shiny hair slicked back, and my classmates would ask me if I was using Brylcreem because my hair shined. Fortunately, in my generation, slicked-back hair was in style. Olive oil was the Greek equivalent of Brylcreem, and who in my generation doesn't remember Brylcreem? I don't know if it was effective, but one thing was certain, as the jingle goes, "A little dab'll do ya."

Komboloi

And that brings me to another topic, komboloi (κομπολοι), Greek worry beads! Greeks will sit and twirl them for hours. What is their origin? I didn't know, but it obviously had something to do with our heritage, so I decided to obtain some facts regarding komboloi.

Komboloi have no religious significance or ceremonial purpose and are used to pass time. Initially, their use by women was frowned upon, but they are now used by both sexes as a fashion accessory and to stop smoking. They represent a symbol of the easygoing Greek mentality and are manipulated to reduce tension. The clicking sound they make when they are moved is thought to have a calming effect. The term komboloi (κομπολογια), "a collection of knots," is derived from κομβος (knot) and λογιο (to say). The term "καθε κομπο προσκευχη λεω" means "at every knot, I say a prayer." The word *komboloi* (κομπολοι) evolved from κομποσκοινι (prayer ropes) and were used by the early Orthodox Christian monks on Mount Athos to keep count as they recited the Jesus prayer. Monks use them with their left hand, leaving their right hand free to make the sign of the cross.

Komboloi generally have an odd number of beads, usually between 17 and 33, often more than a multiple of 4 (4 x 4 + 1), (5 x 4 + 1), or a prime number such as 17, 19, or 23. A prime number is a natural number greater than 1 that has no positive divisors other than 1 and itself. The beads have a head composed of a fixed bead, larger than the others, known as the priest (παπασ); a shield (θυρεους), to separate the two threads and allow the beads to flow freely; and a tassel (φουντα). Initially, komboloi strings had knots. Apparently, the monks on Mount Athos tied knots at intervals on a thick cord to count their prayers. These knotted cords were called komboskini (κομποσκοινι) and were the predecessors to komboloi or beads. These knotted cords had 33 knots to symbolize the age of Christ at the time of his crucifixion.

From a different perspective, the beads represented independence, and each Greek warrior would carry them into battle and would click them as if to emphasize, "I am free; I am Greek." During the 1900s, the beads underwent another change; they were reduced from 33 to 17. The beads are currently made from many different materials and vary in number from 17 to 33 but must always be an odd number. Since three is considered a holy number and since numbers that are divisible by three are considered lucky, komboloi with 27 beads are very desirable.

Greek Superstitions

Greeks, as you are aware, heed many superstitions, and if you weren't exposed to them when you were growing up in my generation, then you weren't brought up Greek. We accepted most of them without question as certainties and normal entities of Greek life, while others appeared to be more inexplicable and peculiar. You will find them amusing, and many of them will revive memories of your childhood and adolescent years as well. Incidentally, to this day, whenever I am confronted with one of these superstitions, I still develop a restlessness, an anxiety that persists until I satisfy its requirement. Bizarre, yes, but I presume that I will always retain that reaction, a sense of Greekness, which is not such a bad quality.

My aunts considered themselves to be multitalented, especially when it came to homeopathic medicine, and in this regard, they were self-anointed

HOMEOPATHIC MEDICINE AND SUPERSTITION

physicians. I am certain it wouldn't startle any of you to know they were exceptional clairvoyants as well. As an example of this unique talent, they possessed the mysterious capability to examine the configuration of coffee grounds within an inverted demitasse coffee cup and, astonishingly, make sweeping predictions about your life. From the grouping of these coffee grounds, they could determine when you were going to take your next trip *and* your destination. Furthermore, because of their outstanding intuitive capacity, they could answer any comprehensive question definitively. You must admit, to be able to accomplish those feats from the positioning of a mass of wet coffee grounds requires an extremely remarkable person with extraordinary predictive powers. And my aunts possessed these talents.

Even more incredible, the limits of their predictive capabilities extended even further. By merely examining your palm, they could make many of the same determinations and predict your life span. Many Greeks, I am sure, walked away from those readings with the fear and even hopeless despair that they faced impending death within the near future.

I remember sitting quietly in astonishment in the kitchen at one of those big round wooden kitchen tables covered with a red-and-white vinyl tablecloth with inverted demitasse coffee cups while my aunt prepared to forecast the future for one of my anxious relatives.

Continuing further into our superstition excursion, and in a different direction, my aunts, as well as many Greeks, consider crows to be bad luck, and even consider them to be harbingers of death. Whenever I was with my aunts in the fields picking dandelions and they would see a crow, I would hear them loudly scream, "Στο καλω, στο καλω, καλα νεα ωα μας φερις!" "Go well into the day and bring me good news!" They would repeat this phrase excitedly several times while waving their arms frantically. It must have worked, because the crows flew away, and my aunts always came home with sacks filled with dandelions.

Strange how these superstitions are ingrained into us during our childhood and how, despite our recognition of them as superstitions as adults, we still preserve their significance. As an example, yesterday I saw a group of crows perched in a tree, and what did I do? Naturally, being a Greek, I instinctively thought of the phrase "στο καλω, στο καλω, καλα νεα να μας φερις!" and despite any logic, I recited it! I remarked, "Crows are bad luck to the Greeks," to those who were with me, to explain my behavior, and so they wouldn't think I had lost all sense of logic.

As Greek children, when we asked for a knife, it was never handed to us directly but instead was placed on the table in front of us by a parent or relative. Old Greeks will never hand someone a knife, since they believe it will cause an argument or a fight. Instead, they will lay it down so that it can be picked up. We were taught to do this at a very young age, and I continue to comply with this compulsion, even though it often results in curious stares. Initially, I attempted to explain the rationale for this behavior by stating, "It's a Greek thing," but now I simply avoid it and ignore the curious stares while I anxiously wait for the person to place the knife on the table. My grandchildren give me puzzled stares when they ask me for a knife and I place it on the table rather than hand it directly to them. I have not attempted to explain the justification of this superstition yet, because I am reluctant to ask them what they think about it.

This next superstition still generates a moderate level of anxiety for me if I ignore it or don't correct it. When removing a pair of shoes, have you ever left one lying on its side or upside down with its sole up? Or have you left them unaligned and not parallel with each other? If you did, were you able to ignore it and continue with your daily routine, or did you feel that something wasn't quite right, that an undefinable apprehension, an uneasiness persisted that was not relieved until its source was identified and corrected? As an example of how powerful this omen is to me, to this day if I discard one of my shoes with its sole up or inverted, or if the shoe is not placed parallel to the other, I develop a restlessness that persists until I return to the closet or wherever the shoe is and turn it upright or align it. It's as if the gods

HOMEOPATHIC MEDICINE AND SUPERSTITION

have compelled me to go back and correct the fault or suffer some unnamed, unpleasant consequence until I rectify the situation.

There must be an obscure shoe god or goddess in Greek mythology, perhaps a relative of Hermes. Nevertheless, whenever I leave a shoe with its sole up or not aligned with its mate, regardless of how irrational the superstition appears to be, and even though I laugh and initially attempt to resist the compulsion, I eventually must turn the shoe right side up. I can be halfway down the street in my car and the compulsion becomes so intense that it forces me to return to make the correction.

Even though my wife will look at me curiously as I satisfy the demands of this compulsion, I don't attempt to explain it to her or anyone else, because it would be difficult for a rational person to understand the power of the Greek shoe god or goddess. I don't know the origin of my "shoe inversion" anxiety, and I am sure it is a feeling that I will never overcome. It most likely originated in my childhood, possibly the result of a command from one of my "goddess aunts" that eventually became driven into my subconscious only to resurface when I began describing it to you. Nevertheless, leaving shoes with their soles up or inverted is a bad omen for the Greeks, and if you experience the same anxiety, please reposition your shoes immediately and say "spit on yourself" or else you risk the persistence of an uncomfortable feeling until the shoes are righted. Incidentally, the same all-inclusive prophylactic phrase can be used if you hear of someone having any misfortune and you don't want the same thing to happen to you.

When you sneeze, Greeks believe someone is talking about you. Furthermore, because of our exceptional insight based on mathematics, we also believe that you can identify that person. Start by having the person who is with you when you sneeze give you a three-digit number. You must then add those numbers together, look through the alphabet until the corresponding letter appears, which gives you the first initial of the person who is talking about you. Obviously, once you have identified that person, you can give him or her the "evil eye!" We Greeks have a mysterious ability to identify the responsible person simply through our physiological response.

According to Greeks, it is a bad omen when two people say the same thing at the same time, and to avoid an argument or a fight, they must both touch something red.

Although this next practice is not used currently, it was customary to cover the eyes of a dead person with coins to prevent them from opening, because it was considered a bad omen if they looked at you. Alternatively, coins placed over the eyes of the deceased provided them with sufficient funds for the boatman to ferry them across the river Styx.

The toast "Yia mas!" (γεια μας) is okay with ouzo, wine, and home-brewed spirits such as tsipouro (τσιπορο), but it is considered bad luck to toast with coffee. This advice is given to all non-Greek guests at the Hartford Hellenic Cultural Center.

Have you ever had guests at your home who would not leave at an appropriate hour? Well, fear not, for the Greeks have a remedy for this situation also. Simply sprinkle salt behind the person that you want to leave your home, and that will chase them out expeditiously.

Now that we have successfully completed the fundamental concepts of homeopathy and superstition, we are able to proceed into advanced superstitions.

The Evil Eye (το κακο ματι)

No story about the Greeks can be complete without a discussion of the evil eye (το κακο ματι). Associating the eyes with the power of the evil eye relates to the belief that the eyes are considered the gateway to the soul, and their expression conveys a multiplicity of emotions. I included it due to its profound historical and cultural significance, and because I fear, if I show disrespect and omit it, that I will become smitten (ματιαζμενος; the correct English translation for ματιαζμενος is "eye catcher," but smitten is commonly used).

HOMEOPATHIC MEDICINE AND SUPERSTITION

One afternoon when I was twelve years old, I was lying on the couch with a headache, and suddenly, without warning, my aunt Migthalou appeared, dressed in her traditional black mourning dress. She bent over me, and with her face about two inches away from mine, began muttering unintelligible phrases in Greek, made the sign of the cross on my forehead and cheeks with oil droplets, and spit into the air three times. She then turned to my mother and nodded her head in the affirmative. Her diagnosis was confirmed. I had been smitten by the evil eye.

It is one thing to hear and read about the evil eye, but it is quite another to live it, and that's what I did many times as I was growing up. The evil eye remains one of the most fascinating aspects of the Greek traditions, because it embraces both facets of religion and history. It is a compelling tradition that perpetuates itself through the ages in the Greek world.

Has anyone ever asked you the significance of that blue bead with the black center pinned to your lapel or fastened to your wristband or bracelet? Have you ever felt uneasy when someone stared at you or looked at you cross-eyed? Suppose someone told you that you looked good or that you had a nice dress, and a few minutes later you spilled coffee all over yourself. You might ask yourself, "How could that have happened?" Well, the Greeks know the answer! They believe it could have been caused by the "evil eye" (το "κακο ματι"), and you may have been the victim of an envious stare.

I don't have to convince you that Greeks are superstitious and that the evil eye is unquestionably the most intriguing and powerful of the Greek superstitions. We are also a very religious people, and the evil eye is deeply rooted in ancient Greece and Greek religion, dating back to the sixth century BC. Given this foundation, it understandably remains a prominent superstition.

Even though there appears to be a contradiction between the Church and laity with respect to the evil eye, they share mutually complementary aspects as well as some common elements. By some accounts, the evil eye has been described as a form of Satanism, while other interpretations suggest that it can be given intentionally or unintentionally and may represent a form of acute jealousy or extreme admiration for a person. This latter explanation implies that the individual casting the evil eye may not necessarily have evil motives but may be envious of someone's superior physical appearance, their riches, or perhaps their strong family bond.

These reasons may be considered adequate for the evil eye to have its effects, and the gaze of someone who harbors feelings of jealousy or envy for things they do not have may result in misfortune to an individual. The receiver of the evil eye is said to be smitten, and this person may experience adversity that manifests in a constellation of difficulties, including financial difficulties, family problems, or a deterioration in health. Severe headache, sadness, feeling of foreboding, hiccups, loss of breath, loss of appetite, vomiting, and aching from head to toe have been associated with the evil eye. Interestingly, the evil eye might also be considered harmful for the person inflicting it as well as for the person upon whom it is inflicted.

The Greek Orthodox Church believes that every evil is the impact of the devil, for only good is derived from God, and that the only means of protection and defense against Satan are the Church's prayers. Satanic powers, the evil eye, known as *vaskania* (βασκανια) by the Greek Orthodox Church, recognizes the jealousy and envy of some people for things they do not possess, such as youth, beauty, and courage.

Vaskania, the evil eye, originates from envy, and the harmful energy that emanates from it is derived from the word "βασκανω," which means to malign, denigrate, or insult. However, the Church believes that a simple look from an envious person causing harm or evil to someone is merely a superstition and a senseless perception, because if this were the case, then at least half the world's population would have been eliminated. If we utilize logic, this theory makes absolute sense. Instead, the Church believes that envy and vaskania are driving forces that cause a behavioral change that may result in injury, and for this reason, the devil and vaskanos are termed "misanthropic."

GREEK ORTHODOX CHURCH-SANCTIONED EXORCISM

The Greek Orthodox Church uses exorcism and the sacrament of baptism to combat satanic powers and to rid possessed individuals of the devil. Baptism is also a method to cleanse the individual of original sin. The exorcism of vaskania by the Greek Orthodox Church and the rite performed against such demonic powers includes a special prayer taken from the ecclesiastical book, the small Euchologion, used exclusively by priests. Other prayers against vaskania are taken from the Megan Hieron Synekdemon (Μεγαν Ιερον Συωεκδημον) book of prayers. Additional prayers used in the exorcism of satanic powers include four prayers of exorcism by Saint John Chrysostom and three prayers by Saint Basil the Great.

As Greeks, we know that there are many aspects of the evil eye and vaskania. One of these is the Church-sanctioned rite to exorcise vaskania, called the Blessing of the Waters. When I was about thirteen years old, I was at home one evening when the doorbell rang. Opening the door, I was astonished to see the Greek priest standing there, because any association with him outside of church was mainly in cases of sickness and death. However, at my father's request, he had arrived to perform the Blessing of the Waters, which at that time I knew nothing about.

He began by immersing a cross in a pan of water that he took from a small vial that he carried with him. He then sprinkled the family and all the rooms with this water to disperse any harmful power and malevolent energy that was present. This rite still is performed and continues to be an important tradition with respect to the expulsion of the evil eye from the Greek home.

However, even though the Greek Orthodox Church encourages its people to pray and exorcise evil, it vigorously rejects secret rites that border on magic, and the Church does not condone rites performed by lay individuals who are attempting to admonish the evil eye. This practice has no relation to the Church's teaching. Lay people's attempts to admonish the evil eye are unacceptable since origins of the evil eye are obscure and based on superstition, ignorance, and no foundation. Given these principles, people who feel that they are under the influence of vaskania must ask to be blessed by a priest.

LAY SECRET RITE OF EXONERATION

Even though the Greek Orthodox Church vigorously rejects secret rites and does not condone rites performed by lay individuals to admonish the evil eye, many Greeks remain steadfast in their belief that it is appropriate for a lay person, typically an old woman—referred to as a ξεματιαδσμα, a person endowed with the ability to admonish the effects of the evil eye—who has been given the special secret rite of exoneration, to recite the prayers to admonish the evil eye. However, if the prayer is revealed indiscriminately, it is understood that the revealer, who is the healer, will likely lose the ability to cast off the evil eye, and that is why the prayer remains so secretive.

Although there are variations in the secret rite and the prayers used by laypersons to admonish the evil eye, the ritual is generally passed to an individual from an older relative of the opposite sex. In most cases, the designated healer or exonerator, who has been taught the secret rite, prepares a vial of olive oil and a small glass of water. She begins the rite by reciting a secret prayer while spitting in the air three times. She then dips a finger in the olive oil and makes the sign of a cross on the receiver's forehead, chin, and both cheeks while letting one drop of oil fall into a glass of holy water (olive oil floats in water because it has a lower density than water). This action is repeated three more times. If the ailment is attributed to the devil, the four drops of oil in the water join to form the ellipsoid shape of an eye, and she recites the prayers while repeating the four signs of the cross. During this time, if the exonerator and the affected individual yawn and the drops of oil in the glass of water disperse or sink to the bottom, the evil eye has been dispelled, and the victim has been exonerated (ξεματιασμενος). However, if the oil continues to float, then the evil eye was not responsible for the ailment. It is critical that the sequence of transmission of the secret prayer be followed,

HOMEOPATHIC MEDICINE AND SUPERSTITION

or the ability to cast off the evil eye is lost. (The good number is three, and the best number is nine. The person is prayed over three times and then three more times, totaling nine.)

In certain cases, it is not necessary for the person smitten by the evil eye to be present to be exonerated. Clothing from such an individual may be taken to an exorcist, and the sufferer will become well again.

The prayers to exorcise the evil eye were taught to me, but out of respect for the Church as the only legitimate institution to exorcise satanic powers, and admittedly, partly because I am fearful that I would lose the capability to expel the evil eye if I revealed them, they will not be included in this discussion. Even though I recognize the Greek Orthodox Church as the only legitimate source of expelling Satan and understand that the Church rejects secret rites designed to expel the devil as superstition, there is a part of me, based perhaps on my sense of Greekness, that makes me a skeptic. Nevertheless, even though I have been taught the rite, I have never performed a lay exorcism.

The oil and water used in the rite of the evil eye is obtained during Holy Week. Symbolically, on Holy Thursday, the day Jesus was crucified, the body of Christ was left on the cross in the church overnight. This was the only time that Christ's body was accessible to the parishioners who left containers of oil and salt and retrieved them as holy items on Friday morning. The holy water was received several days later when Christ appeared to his disciples after the resurrection. We keep these holy objects in an iconostasion (εικονοστασιον), a small shelf hung on the wall. On the shelf is traditionally an icon of the Virgin Mary, as well as holy objects blessed by the Church.

To be grammatically correct, the term *κακο ματι*, when translated, means "bad eye," not "evil eye." As a child, I was constantly aware of the evil eye and was warned about it by my parents and relatives. There were even instances, for reasons unknown to me, when I was told that I had been smitten by the eye, but I don't think I ever understood the implication of it at that time.

As a child, I experienced frequent bloody noses, the etiology of which remained unknown. Following several physician consultations with no explanation or results, my father appealed to his cousin, my aunt Migthalou (θιτσα Μιγδαλου), the local exonerator, who was endowed with the extraordinary capability of dispelling the evil eye. Following a brief consultation, she advised him that there was no doubt that I was smitten and that I should be brought to her so that the eye could be dispelled. The exoneration to rid the evil eye and eliminate my epistaxis (nosebleed) was about to begin.

Without hesitation, I was brought to my aunt's home, and as I sat in her sunlit kitchen anxiously waiting for the spiritual therapeutic regimen to start and watching her prepare for the ritual, I thought, *If whoever cast the evil eye on me were here and could see my aunt, he would release the spell on me immediately and run.*

Despite being especially gentle at first appearance, my aunt was an imposing figure. She was a heavy, buxom lady, with several conspicuous thick black hairs extending above her upper lip and from her chin. Below her thick silver-black monobrow, she had two large, almond-colored eyes that expressed tenderness, reinforced by a wide, gentle smile that extended from her rosy cheeks. Her gray-silver hair was knotted in a bun atop her head, and hanging from her neck was a heavy gold chain that supported a large gold cross that stretched almost to the waist of her black-and-gray-checkered mourning outfit. Her waist was discernible only by a tightly cinched white apron tied in the back with a huge knot.

Having prepared for the ritual, she approached me and began. She muttered several lengthy but barely audible Greek phrases through her yellowed teeth, and she spat three times while rolling her eyeballs upward to gaze at the heavens. I didn't know what to think, so I sat there transfixed and bewildered. After a few seconds, from a vial containing olive oil, she anointed my forehead, chin, and cheeks three times while allowing a drop of oil to fall into a glass of water in front of me each time. Following a short prayer in Greek, the ritual was completed, and the evil eye was purportedly dispelled.

Only one problem remained, however. I continued to get bloody noses. If you knew my aunt as well as I did, you would be surprised, because one glance at her would make you believe that if she could not exorcise the evil eye by ritual, then she could probably do it by casting a stern glance in its direction.

Another and rather amusing example of the evil eye occurred when I was sixteen years old and an usher for a good friend at a Greek wedding in Boston, Massachusetts. As we were dressing in the hotel room prior to the wedding ceremony and departing for the church, the ushers, as is customary, began toasting the groom with ouzo, a fiery Greek liquor. Even though I was the youngest of the ushers and had never tasted ouzo prior to this, I thought it would be in poor taste and even bad luck if I refrained from the toast. Being excited, and complicated by my not having had anything to eat that morning, the stage was set for the evil eye. The toast, "γεια σου" (to your long life), given by the best man, and my subsequent drink, was abruptly followed by a flame that burned intensely as it made its gradual descent to Hades but eventually moderated to smoldering embers that continued to persist. Shortly thereafter, we proceeded to the church, and everything appeared to be manageable, even though the caldera continued to smolder.

Greek weddings consist of several steps—blessing of the rings, lighting of the candles, drinking from the common cup, and the crowning of the bride and groom. The priest crosses the crowns (στεφανα) over the couple's heads three times, then places them on their heads and leads the newly married couple and the best man in a counterclockwise representative dance-like procession called the "Isaia Horeve" (Ισαια Χορεβε; translated means "the Dance of Isaiah"). They circle three times around a small table, marking their first movements as a couple and proclaiming their marriage. Thanks to the evil eye, I never saw the crowns placed on their heads nor did I see those ceremonial first steps as a married couple. Instead of experiencing that joyful moment, I felt a rush of intense heat erupt in my head, and the caldera on Thera that had been smoldering finally exploded. I apparently reached the point of no return.

The next thing I remember was sitting on the tar in the church parking lot propped up against the front tire of a car in bright sunlight, feeling completely disoriented. Staring at me from a few inches away was an old lady I had never seen before, who was obviously one of the wedding guests, dressed in a traditional Greek black mourning dress (yes, even at a wedding). Without hesitation, she began to recite the prayers for the evil eye as I sat there, bewildered. Within a few seconds, I realized what had happened. I must have been smitten. Can you imagine how fortunate I was to be at an event that was also attended by an admonisher of the evil eye? Without hesitation, she proceeded to exonerate the evil eye, and apart from an initial embarrassment, the remainder of the wedding went well.

PREVENTION AGAINST THE EVIL EYE

While we are discussing the evil eye, if you have any torn items of clothing, it may be disadvantageous to discard them, because the Greeks believe that any degree of imperfection makes you a less attractive target as far as the evil eye is concerned. Leaving the house with a torn sock, as an example, may be advantageous if you are worried about being smitten by the evil eye, because a torn sock will make it less likely that someone will be envious of you, and that will decrease the possibility that you will be smitten. I give my wife this convenient excuse whenever I attempt to leave the house wearing a worn piece of clothing, so I don't have to take the time to change. Despite that logic, it generally isn't effective, and her typical response is that maybe I *should* be smitten.

The following ritual to ward off the evil eye is one of my favorites. Have you ever been in the presence of Greeks, and suddenly, for no apparent obvious reason, one woman spits on another woman? Horrified, you eventually learn that the woman who was spat on was complimented by another woman in the group. Therefore, to ward off the evil eye in this circumstance, the person who gave the compliment is required to spit three times on the complimented person, since spitting three times is apparently insulting enough to negate the compliment and prevent the curse of the evil eye, supposedly chasing the devil away. To finalize this rite, the person who gave the compliment should make a puff of breath through pursed lips as if spitting, an action that further protects the recipient from getting the evil eye.

Greek weddings are among the most beautiful Orthodox ceremonies. The bride, elegantly dressed, is escorted by her father down the aisle, when suddenly several Greek women are likely to lean over from their pews and spit in the bride's direction three times. If you aren't familiar with this ritual, most likely you will think they are deliberately attempting to insult her. Despite this reaction, she and her father continue to stroll down the aisle unconcernedly. The explanation? Obviously, someone at the wedding must have described how beautiful the bride was, and to prevent her from being smitten by the evil eye, the spitting ritual is required.

And there's more. If you are aware that a compliment has been given to you, and you are worried that you might have been smitten by the evil eye, you can utter the word "garlic" (σκορδο) under your breath, spit on yourself three times, and have the person who paid you the compliment spit on you three times also. These practices continue to be encouraged today in many Greek communities, especially by older-generation Greeks.

EVIL EYE GIVERS

Although Greeks believe that the evil eye can be given by anyone, they suspect that people with certain characteristics remain more likely to deliver it. Individuals with visibly defective eyes, eyes blackened by trauma, or who have eyebrows that meet are often accused of casting the evil eye. Old women are also believed to possess the ability to deliver the evil eye. People with the ability to exorcise the evil eye are apparently endowed with the genetics to live to a very old age.

From my experience, many of my aunts satisfied this latter criterion. Since light-colored eyes are less common in the Mediterranean, people with green or blue eyes are considered more likely to deliver the evil eye intentionally or unintentionally, so beware when a blue-eyed person pays you a compliment; it could be disastrous. This is one explanation for why the evil eye amulets are blue; an alternative explanation is that blue symbolizes heaven or godliness, and Greeks believe that blue keeps evil away. Many Greek structures in Greece, especially in the Cyclades, such as doors, window frames, and domes, are painted turquoise blue. And in the United States, many Greek Orthodox Church domes are painted turquoise blue.

TALISMANS

The Greek Orthodox Church does not recognize the use of words or prayers by laypersons to dispel the evil eye, nor does it condone the use of amulets or other objects that are contrived to prevent the evil eye, because they portray magic. Anything beyond the Church's prayers constitutes a denial of faith, and whoever uses exorcisms or talismans shows lack of faith and impiety toward God. The Church does, however, consider the cross to be an acceptable talisman and regards that faith in God, communion, and confession are the most beneficial talismans the Church can offer. According to Orthodoxy, the Church is our talisman, and it encourages us to avoid any non-ecclesiastical means of sanctification, since it exploits insecurity and is usually simply a moneymaker.

Despite the Church's opinion on the rites of lay exorcism and the use of talismans, and because the evil eye is rooted in ancient Greece and Greek religion, it remains a prominent superstition, and carrying some form of the evil eye continues to be a vigorous practice among many Greeks. Jewelry known as atropaic (ατροφικη), the Greek word for prophylactic—including necklaces, bracelets, rings, talismans, and amulets in the form of blue eyes—is typically worn.

As an example, I had a small, triangular-shaped cloth pouch, called a talisman, folded over itself several times. It contained a clove of garlic or a holy item, such as crushed dried flowers from the Easter service or candle wax

HOMEOPATHIC MEDICINE AND SUPERSTITION

from Church, and was pinned into my right pants pocket when I was young. This practice is called "ασημο το φυλαχτο" ("silver the talisman"). A young child is given "silver," usually coins, or a talisman for good luck.

Depending on the region in Greece, many methods are used to ward off the evil eye. It is not unusual to see garlic strung over the front door or a cactus plant in a doorway threshold placed as a talisman against the evil eye. My aunt Harriet had a cactus plant on her windowpane in her kitchen. Cactus plants protect against evil. I always wondered why the plant was there, and now I know the reason.

The belief is that babies, children, and women are common targets for the evil eye, although men certainly are not excluded. In addition to a gold cross, I wear an evil eye leather wrist bracelet, and my daughter and grandchildren wear one as well. Although I am not superstitious, I wear it more as a tradition and as a symbol of my Greekness, and when someone notices it, I am eager to explain its history and significance.

Following my mother's death, while I was cleaning out her apartment and packing her clothes to be given to charitable organizations, I opened her dresser drawer and found a brassiere with a small, neatly folded, cloth-covered clove of garlic pinned to it. It was a talisman. Pinned neatly against the talisman was a carefully folded twenty-dollar bill. I laughed affectionately when I saw the money, because I know it provided her with a sense of security, however slight. Nonetheless, I quickly realized that I also carry a twenty-dollar bill secured to a credit card with an elastic band in my wallet apart from my other bills. It makes no sense, since it could be included with the rest of the bills, but its exclusion apparently provides me with a sense of security. Go figure.

CHAPTER 9

Religious Holidays and Events

"With the Greek family, holidays and events are chaos"

MUCH OF THE GREEK LIFE and many traditions are centered around the Greek Orthodox Church and faith. For Greeks, religious holidays are social events celebrated with extended family members and friends. Planning for a successful family holiday is extensive and is evidenced by a heightened activity level requiring participation by all family members. Greek women will work tirelessly preparing a variety of appetizers and main dishes to be served to the "family." Greek men will ensure that the assortment of liquor is adequate and abundant and will order special cuts of fresh meats. Moreover, a family member must make sure that Uncle Ted is available to play his bouzouki. But which uncle Ted? There are six of them, and they all play the bouzouki. Many Greek holiday events overflow to the outdoors, so prayers must be recited to ensure good weather.

Certain specific rituals have been imbedded so deeply that I continue to observe them out of respect for Orthodoxy. As an example, it is not unusual to see a person crossing themselves as they pass in front of an Orthodox Church. This ritual extends back to childhood when Greek parents, schoolteachers, priests, and relatives repeatedly emphasized the importance of this behavior until it became spontaneous. Over time, the religious significance of this practice is so penetrating that it has resulted in a compulsive behavior. Failure to observe this tradition results in a persistent anxiety relieved only by making the appropriate remedial action, which is to return to the church and make the sign of the cross.

This has happened to me on several occasions, and when it did, I turned the car around, drove by the church again, made the sign of the cross, and my apprehension went away. Perhaps this serves as an example of the Greek psychiatric explanation for the expiation of guilt. In another example, as children, we were taught never to cross our legs or feet while we were in church, and most Greeks of my generation will readily admit that if they inadvertently cross their legs while in church, they quickly make the imbedded postural adjustment.

Easter

Without question, Greek Orthodox Easter is the principal religious holiday in the Greek Orthodox calendar. Because of its significance, I thought it would be appropriate to chronicle the events as they occur and to include a number of personal anecdotes that may be appropriate as we continue to appreciate its significance and understand the miracle of the resurrection of Jesus Christ and the magnificence of Orthodoxy.

The Greek Orthodox faith follows the modified Julian calendar to establish the date for Easter, and since that date must fall after Passover, it does not always coincide with Easter of other faiths. Orthodox Easter falls on the first Sunday after the full moon of the spring equinox.

The Easter holiday season begins with the Carnival season (Αποκριες) that traditionally begins ten weeks before Greek Orthodox Easter and culminates on the weekend before Clean Monday, the first day of the Great Lent. It is three weeks long. The roots of the Carnival go back to the days of worshipping Dionysius, the god of wine. During this period, the Greeks celebrate Halloween. When I was young, my aunt Mary dressed my cousin Teddy and me as little girls, dressed herself as a man, and took us out to her friends' homes. Naturally, the friends had to be Greek, because anyone else would not understand what we were doing, since traditional Halloween was still several months away. My mother and father could not stop laughing at the sight of the three of us standing in the doorway in our costumes.

Meat fare Sunday, also known as the Sunday of the Last Judgment, is the third Sunday of a three-week period prior to the commencement of Great Lent. It is the last day that eating meat is permitted until Easter. The following Sunday is known as Cheesefare Sunday (τιροφαγος), also called Forgiveness Sunday, which is the Sunday before the Sunday of Orthodoxy, the last day prior to the commencement of Lent. No eggs or dairy products are eaten after Cheesefare Sunday. Great Lent begins on Clean Monday (καθαρη δευτερα), seven weeks before Easter Sunday, and it culminates on Easter Sunday. Clean Monday, also known as Ash Monday (analogous to Ash Wednesday, the beginning of Lent for Western Christianity), marks the beginning of a forty-day fasting period and represents the forty days Jesus spent fasting in the desert.

Clean Monday implies that Christians should clean up their spiritual houses and begin the holy season with clean hearts and good intentions. It also is a day of strict fasting, and Christians are not allowed to eat from midnight to noon and cannot have any meat. The typical menu for Clean Monday includes tarama salata (ταραμα σαλατα), derived from carp or cod, stuffed grape leaves, halva for dessert, and of course, a homemade liquor called tsipouro (τσιπουρο)—a strong pomace-based drink containing 40 to 45 percent alcohol. Clean Monday (Καθαρη Δευτερα) also marks the first day of spring and signifies an end to the preceding Carnival celebrations. It is a Greek holiday and is one of the most festive days of the year. Greeks celebrate it with outdoor activities and picnics.

Clean Monday is followed by Great Lent (Μεγαλι Σαρακοστη), a time of fasting and abstaining from foods and other products from animals with red blood, as well as fish and seafood with backbones.

Great Lent concludes on Saturday before Palm Sunday and is known as Lazarus Saturday. On this day, the resurrection of Saint Lazarus from the dead is celebrated, symbolizing the promise of universal resurrection.

Palm Sunday, also known as "The Triumphant Entry," celebrates the triumphant entrance of Jesus into Jerusalem. The palms symbolize goodness and victory; they were placed in his path as he entered Jerusalem on a donkey prior to his arrest on Holy Thursday and his crucifixion on Good Friday.

Holy Week has great religious significance for the Greeks, and it concludes Sunday morning at midnight with the resurrection of Christ. Because of its religious importance, I have included a brief description of the historical events of this period, culminating with the miracle of Christ's resurrection. Holy Monday commemorates the "withering of the fig tree." The Bible describes a fig tree with leaves but devoid of fruit, symbolizing that many people claim to have ethical and religious identities but, in reality, have empty lives that yield no fruit. Holy Tuesday represents the anointing of Christ with myrrh by the leper woman. The sacred ceremony of the mystery of the holy unction is celebrated on Holy Wednesday, and the priest anoints the parishioners with holy oil, which symbolizes the visible carrier of the grace of God.

On Holy Thursday, Christ's last instructions were given to his disciples during the last supper, and twelve gospels are read. A Greek Orthodox tradition on Holy Thursday is that eggs are dyed red, symbolizing that the Virgin Mary dyed the eggs red to represent the blood of Christ.

From the church bell tower on Good Friday, a solitary bell rings once every thirty seconds throughout the day and continues to distribute its message of supreme sorrow by providing a solemn reminder of Christ's death. That I was able to play a small role in delivering that message as a child is something I will never forget. As altar boys, we rang the church bell manually every thirty seconds throughout the day. To accomplish this, we had to climb up a precarious flight of indoor stairs that led to a small rectangular trapdoor in the third-floor ceiling of the church. On the other side was an unsteady outdoor ladder that led to a confining outdoor bell tower approximately four stories high. Those were the days before technology was available to make the bell ring automatically. Nevertheless, we willingly performed this task in pairs, but it wasn't long before I knew where the term "bats in the belfry" came from. The clanging sound every thirty seconds was deafening, and the vibration probably caused some of my fillings to loosen. Nonetheless, it was a unique experience, and despite its somber significance, when the sky was clear, the view from that height was spectacular.

Below us, within the church proper, a group of Greek women, mostly elderly, dressed in their traditional black outfits, and many who had remained in Church overnight since Holy Thursday to symbolically protect the body of Christ, began diligently preparing Christ's tomb (επιταφιον) for the Good Friday (Μεγαλη Παρασκευη) service. A laborious daylong project that began early in the morning following an overnight vigil and finally concluded in time for the afternoon church service, it entailed a meticulous placement of thousands of flowers that completely covered the tomb. These women, adhering to a long, strict Lenten fast in accordance to Orthodox tradition, prepared the epitafion, a cloth bearing the image of the dead body of Christ. They ate only plain bread and olives and drank vinegar, the latter of which represented the vinegar-filled sponge thrust up to Christ on the end of a Roman spear while he was on the cross. Remarkably, none of these women, some of whom were elderly and frail, developed a hypoglycemic reaction and collapsed. This Spartan meal was also made available to the bell ringers, and we ate it without hesitation. I remember that it gave us an attachment and a feeling of participation in the holy event as it developed. On Good Friday afternoon, the body of Christ was removed from the cross and wrapped in a white cloth by the priest, who carried it protectively to the altar.

The Good Friday evening church service, beginning with the lamentations of the tomb, is considered by most Greeks, as well as non-Greeks who have witnessed it, to be among the most beautiful and poignant religious services they have ever observed, and it is difficult for me to describe it without becoming emotional. Within the church, the air is filled with the scent of flowers that drape the sepulcher, and there is a stillness, an uneasy calm, as parishioners congregate and sit quietly facing the epitafion.

The Good Friday service begins in the somber church when the priest and choir, robed in black vestments, begin to chant the lamentations of the tomb, a passionate and deeply moving expression of grief. As a compelling reminder of the significance of the moment, a large, wooden, vacant crucifix draped in a black shroud stands alone to the right of the priest. The epitaphios (επιταφιο), the cloth representation of Christ, is taken from the altar by the priest and placed in the sepulcher while the parishioners hold lit candles with red cups that signify the death of Christ and his descent into Hades. As the epitaphios is placed in the sepulcher, the parishioners and the choir sing hymns of praise, and the priest sprinkles the sepulcher and the entire congregation with fragrant holy water. At this point, the lamentations are transferred from Christ to lamenting for our own sins, as we are reminded that we are far from God. The Good Friday service, in addition to being passionate, is impactful and has a personal meaning for every parishioner.

Regardless of the solemnity of the Good Friday church service, inevitably there are humorous moments. One incident occurred when we were altar boys that could have been catastrophic had it not been for the alertness of the deacon, who had been chanting as the priest was preparing to read from the Gospel. Chris, Louie, and I, performing our duties as altar boys, were standing at attention with lit candles adjacent to the priest when, suddenly, the back of Louie's vestment ignited in a small flame. Louie was unaware of it, but Chris's eyes immediately shifted to the potential catastrophe, and I can still remember his horrified expression. But what recourse did we have? The Bible was being read, and we had to maintain our respectful positions. Fortunately, the deacon rushed over and extinguished the flames before Louie realized what had happened. When the Gospel was concluded, Louie walked to the altar with a severely burned and smoldering vestment—the perils of being an altar boy.

As children, we were told to be cautious when in crowds and not to play with matches. The danger from fire inevitably presents itself in a crowd, especially when the individuals in that crowd are holding lit candles. However, the Good Friday church service presented potential dangers unavoidable because of religious tradition.

Typically, on Sundays and for many religious holiday services, it is not difficult to find a place to sit in the church. This, however, is not characteristic of Good Friday. On this most solemn day, many "good" Orthodox Christians suddenly remember their religious commitment and feel a compulsion to attend the evening service. Fulfillment of this religious obligation is virtuous, but from a physical perspective and safety issue, the church's capacity is exceeded, resulting in a serious fire code violation.

The church quickly becomes filled with parishioners. Most are stuffed into pews, while some stand cramped in aisles, and others are squeezed into whatever space they can fit. But this is not merely an issue of overcrowding, which is a fire code violation in itself. They all hold lit candles dripping with wax. Regardless of the impending laundry costs incurred by wax solidifying onto jackets and coats, this chaotic scene is a potential fire hazard. Even though we are in the protective sanctity of the church, I identify the location of the exits.

Once, during the Good Friday evening service, an adorable elderly couple was sitting attentively in the pew in front of me. The lady, who was rather short and stout, was wearing a heavy brown wool coat with a black fur collar and a black hat, from which extended a veil. She clutched a black pocketbook in her left hand, leaving her right hand free to make the sign of the cross. Her husband, who was thin and about four inches shorter, was wearing a gray-black overcoat. At the point in the service when the priest exclaimed that Christ had died, the husband turned to his wife and said, "Better him than me" (καλυτερα απο τον εαυτο μου). Hearing that comment, she swiftly turned, glared at him for an instant, and then swung her pocketbook and hit him in the shoulder. Greeks, despite the seriousness of the moment, do have a funny side!

The lamentations of Christ are especially emotional, and the significance of this segment of the Good Friday service is especially impactful, as characterized by the somberness of the parishioners' faces. When the lamentations conclude, the sepulcher is carried around the exterior periphery of the church. At that time, six church members approach and pick up the heavy, flower-draped wooden sepulcher, struggle to lift and support it on their shoulders, and proceed to slowly carry it down the main church aisle to the front entrance while waiting for the priest, who sprays the parishioners with holy water.

The six men are usually members of the church council and are not necessarily the strongest or the sturdiest individuals. A few years ago, a near-catastrophic incident occurred involving an older, distinguished council member. He was supporting the front end of the sepulcher, and as he attempted to descend the front steps of the church, his knee collapsed, and the sepulcher lurched forward. Suddenly, everyone gasped in horror as the remaining council members struggled to prevent it from falling to the ground. Miraculously, he regained his stability, the sepulcher was stabilized, and he completed his assignment.

From the front entrance of the church, called the narthex, the priest, the altar boys, and the choir, still singing, follow the sepulcher as it is taken outside and carried around the periphery of the church, followed by the parishioners with lit candles. At four points along the route, symbolic of the cross, the procession stops, and the priest recites a special prayer before the procession proceeds once again until it reaches the narthex of the church.

At this point, the sepulcher bearers maintain its elevated position, and the altar boys, the choir, and finally the parishioners kneel and walk under it until everyone enters the church once again. The procession takes about one hour. When the service is completed, the priest distributes a flower to each parishioner, and they attempt to keep their candle lit on the way home. It is easy to distinguish a person of the Orthodox faith on Good Friday evening by the lit candles glowing in their cars.

On Holy Saturday (Μεγαλο Σαββατο), Greeks traditionally prepare the lamb for the Easter dinner to be eaten after midnight mass and later on Easter Sunday. The lamb is generally placed on a spit (σουβλα) and basted with lemon juice, herbs, and spices. Depending on the location in Greece, the lamb may be baked in ovens surrounded by potatoes that simmer in the juice. The religious significance of lamb dates to the Old Testament when God commanded that Abraham sacrifice his son. Abraham dutifully obeyed, and while preparing for the sacrifice, God stopped him, and Abraham sacrificed a lamb instead. Historically, the ancient Greeks sacrificed a lamb to atone for their sins. Moreover, because Christ died on the cross for our sins, he has become the sacrificial lamb. Roasted lamb is served in honor of Christ, the Lamb of God who was sacrificed and rose again on Easter. Easter, then, is the day when Christians commemorate Jesus's sacrifice, and lamb is eaten in remembrance of this selfless act. (Incidentally, of biblical interest, John the Baptist was the first person to refer to Jesus as the Lamb of God.)

I will always remember the years when we would arrive at my uncle Chris's house early on Holy Saturday morning to prepare for Easter. While my mother and aunts were cooking in the kitchen, my uncle Chris and several of my uncles and cousins busily dug a pit in his backyard and filled it with coals in preparation for the lamb roast. When I think back to those times, I can only imagine what my uncle's neighbors must have thought as they looked out and saw us with picks and shovels feverishly digging a hole in the early morning mist just before sunrise. It had all the characteristics of a crime scene taken from a mobster movie. There we were, four or five of us, hovering over a hole in the ground, digging furiously until one of my uncles determined that it was deep enough. To an anxious neighbor, I'm sure they must have been thinking, deep enough for what? Eventually, when they finally saw the lamb being carried out on a large tray and placed on the spit, I am certain their apprehension turned to relief. For us, it was a natural thing to do.

My uncle Chris would roast the lamb on a spit, meticulously rotating it by hand every few minutes while several of my uncles and cousins would stand nearby, preparing to offer advice regarding its preparation time, seasoning, and rotation speed. Despite the early morning hour, beer or wine rather than coffee was their beverage of choice. And why not? It was a special event that required appropriate beverages to sharpen the mind for this most important task. However, as most of you know, whenever Greeks congregate to complete an assignment, the prospects of disagreement developing into a heated discussion range from excellent to absolute—especially if they are influenced by the nectar of the gods. Within seconds, any one of them could become kindled by an ember from the fire pit, and that could ignite them into a fiery debate about the lamb's preparation or about anything else, for that matter. Even worse, since, as you know, Greeks argue with their arms and hands as well as their mouths, if my uncle Chris, the chief spit rotator, would enter the fray and forget to rotate the spit, the animated discussion could easily turn the Easter lamb into charcoal.

When the lamb was finally roasted, it was removed from the spit, placed on a large baking tray, and carried into the kitchen by the victorious Spartans. Nonetheless, those unpretentious events, with relatives that I love, provided me with lifelong happy memories of my Greekness. After the lamb was prepared and the table set for dinner, we would attend midnight mass on Holy Saturday.

Just before midnight during the Great Saturday night church service (Μεγαλο Σαββατο), with the priest and the choir dressed in black vestments, the lamentations of the tomb are repeated. Just before midnight, the Orthos of the Resurrection begins, and all the lights in the church except an eternal flame are turned off, symbolizing the darkness within the tomb. During this brief interval, not a sound is heard in the church. At precisely midnight, the priest emerges from the altar wearing white vestments and carrying two lit candles and the holy light (αγιο φως), and proclaims that Christ has risen! (Χριστος Ανεστε!) He then passes the holy light to the parishioners, who reply, "Yes, it

RELIGIOUS HOLIDAYS AND EVENTS

is true, He has risen!" (αληθος ανεστε!) Ultimately, the whole church radiates with joy and with light, and the safety code is overextended again.

When the midnight service is concluded, the burning candles are taken home, and the carbon from the flame is used to burn the sign of the cross on the door, a symbol of good luck for the next year. Any non-Greek who sees that sign might become confused regarding its significance. No, it is not intended to ward off zombies. Everyone knows that is what garlic is intended for!

The term *midnight mass* is misleading, however, since the service begins at 10:00 p.m. and ends following an Easter sermon at approximately at 1:00 a.m. This is another classic example of Greek time, and without question, midnight mass is a testament to endurance, and completion is reserved for the stout hearted, although many parishioners attempt to persevere.

Once, when a few of my friends and I were serving as altar boys, with only a few moments to go before the end of midnight mass, we were holding candles while the priest was reading from the Bible. Suddenly and unexpectedly, we heard a thunderous crash that came from one of the pews. Without turning my head, I glanced to my left and saw a woman with two heavy thick-heeled black shoes attached to black nylon-covered legs knotted below the knees being quickly carried from the church. I never questioned if she had passed out because of the evil eye, the lateness of the hour, or low blood sugar levels attributed to several days of fasting.

No Greek will argue with you that the Easter midnight service is a marathon (as Mr. Portokalos would say, "The word *marathon* comes from the Greek ..."). When I was younger, the typical midnight Easter service would conclude between 1:00 and 2:00 a.m. Because we were altar boys, we had to stay until the conclusion of that epic service, and that included the post liturgical sermon as well, but as I observed, immediately after the priest proclaimed, "Christ has risen," at midnight, most parishioners would quickly escape, leaving only the resolute few to remain until the service concluded. One year, to prevent this premature exodus, the resolute priest ordered the church council members to lock the doors—another fire hazard. A few days later, following a telephone call to the fire marshal, I suppose from a disgruntled and anonymous parishioner, that situation was quickly resolved, and the "spiritual doors" remained open. More recently, however, the length of the grueling midnight mass has been abbreviated, enabling the parishioners to satisfy their hunger earlier.

Easter is the first time since the beginning of Great Lent that Greeks have no dietary restrictions. Following the midnight service, and before going home to eat roasted lamb, many parishioners will customarily sit down in the church community center to have *magiritsa (μαγειρίτσα)*, Easter lamb soup. Even though my best friend would look forward to his annual Easter midnight magiritsa, I would always go directly home following the service. Despite its significance, I could never fortify myself to try it. Magiritsa is served to break the forty-day Great Lent, and traditionally, this is the only time when it is served. It is often accompanied by sweet Easter bread called *tsoureki (τσουρέκι)*, which has a red egg in its center.

Greeks believe that lamb served in this manner eases the gastrointestinal system back to its normal state from an extended period of fasting, improving the ability to digest red meat again. The variations of magiritsa depend on the region of Greece that you are from. The parts of the lamb that are generally used are the innards and include the heart, lungs, liver, and intestines. The rest of the lamb is put on a spit and roasted on Easter Sunday. In Thessaly, the region of Greece where I am from, it is not served as a soup but is fricasseed and prepared with a large variety of vegetables, but without onions or rice.

Also, following the resurrection of Christ, Greeks will crack red eggs with each other while proclaiming "Christ has risen." The egg is the symbol for the renewal of life, and cracking it symbolizes Christ's resurrection and his breaking free of the tomb. Traditionally, whoever remains with the intact eggshell will have good luck for a year.

The fifty days following Easter are known as the *pentekostarion (πεντηκοστάριον)*. This represents a period dedicated to the belief that God is our companion and is present in our daily life and thoughts. This concept should be paramount every day throughout our lives. But how quickly we forget.

Easter is the most significant holiday for the Greeks. The resurrection of Christ symbolizes a rebirth for all Greeks. Moreover, it represents an opportunity for them to evaluate their lives as well as to formulate their future. It is a joyous holiday, proclaiming the miracle of life.

The Rite of Baptism

The rite of Baptism is an especially important religious rite within the Greek Orthodox Church. It generally occurs between forty days and one year after birth. Before the baby is immersed, the priest blesses the water in the baptismal font and adds myrrh (olive oil blessed by the patriarch). The infant is given to the priest by the godparents. The baby, undressed and wrapped in a white towel, is then immersed three times into the font by the priest while he repeats the baby's name three times. The child is then dressed in white clothes, and traditionally, a gold chain with a cross is placed around the baby's neck by the priest, and the child receives the first holy communion. When the ceremony concludes, the parents of the child traditionally kiss the hands of the godparents, wish a long life to the baby, and then celebrate the event with a party.

When a child is born, or baptized, it is Greek tradition to give that child either silver or gold coins, ensuring that they will continue to have security throughout life. Following this tradition, I gave my nephews and my grandchildren several silver dollars shortly after they were born. Similarly, when giving someone a wallet as a gift, traditionally, a Greek will always include a coin. (The Greeks believe that money attracts money and, therefore, a Greek should always have a coin in his pocket. Whenever we visited my uncle Bill, he would always put a few coins in my pocket. Now I know why, and I continue to wait for that tradition to be fulfilled.)

Other Greek Holidays

When I was growing up, Greeks seemed to have more holidays than anyone else. And in accordance with tradition, we were expected to attend all the events and congregate at one of my aunt's houses, typically my aunt Harriet's house, for a celebration that would begin in early afternoon and extend into the evening. Moreover, I would wear a white shirt and a necktie and would be expected to behave as an adult. In the meantime, many of my friends would be playing baseball or enjoying other seasonal activities. But not if you were a Greek kid. The only consolation was that all my Greek friends were celebrating the same way I was.

Within Greek families, it was tradition that we spent most of the Greek holidays with the eldest aunt and uncle and their family as a sign of respect. The only problem with that is the gathering included at least thirty Greeks, many who came from all parts of New Hampshire. There were relatives everywhere, and many of them with the same names. At least this made it easier for me, since I didn't have to remember different names.

The kitchen was filled with my aunts, most in black mourning outfits, all speaking and gesturing wildly at the same time, reminiscent of a flock of crows, each one brandishing a thick wooden spoon with an apron tied securely around her waist, the uniform of the day. I will always remember the sound of their thick-heeled black shoes resonating authoritatively over the linoleum floor; they reminded me of military generals, each with a compelling opinion about how the dinner should be made, how much seasoning should be used, and when it should be served. From such a seemingly uncoordinated effort bordering on chaos, it seemed miraculous that anything could be accomplished.

Moreover, because of the work proceeding and the ovens stretched to their maximum power, the kitchen resembled a sauna. Cognizant of this pandemonium and fearing a reprimand for trespassing on sacred culinary territory, my uncles and cousins dispersed into adjacent rooms to escape.

As this chaos was proceeding in the kitchen during one Thanksgiving afternoon, I was watching television in the adjacent living room with my two older cousins, Charlie and Greg, when they decided it would be a good idea to play basketball by throwing tightly wrapped paper balls into a circular yellow-white light fixture that hung from the ceiling. As the game started, the commotion provoked my aunt Harriet to temporarily pause from her kitchen leadership command to investigate. When she looked up and saw those paper balls, apparently by their shadows within the fixture, we were subjected to a lengthy and heated reprimand, and the game was abruptly terminated.

The Greek Orthodox Church is a powerful influential factor in most Greek holidays. As an example, each day of the year is dedicated to a Christian saint, and if you are named after one of them, that day is designated as your name day. To the Greeks, name days are more important than birthdays and other holidays, and in their celebration, it is customary that a Greek family open their home to family and friends and acknowledge the celebrant by providing appetizers and drinks. Greeks believe that celebrating a name day brings you closer to God, providing an additional example of the closeness of the extended Greek family.

Greeks named Chris celebrate their name day on Christmas Day. Many of the same family members that congregated at my aunt's home on Thanksgiving, in addition to other friends as well, would visit my uncle Chris's home on Christmas Day. He lived in a new yellow Cape Cod home on the west side of the city. And of course, because this was a new home, it had a living room rather than a parlor, but maintaining tradition, it had clear plastic-covered furniture and doilies everywhere.

Because of the large number of relatives and friends that came to celebrate his name day, my uncle arranged several folding chairs in a circle in their small living room that would quickly become filled with exuberant Greeks flailing their arms while noisily discussing Greek politics and local Greek issues. I would sit there for what seemed like hours, wondering what I was doing there except watching my aunts' ankles swell even further.

The issue that appeared most prominent and that occupied the most discussion was the popularity or unpopularity of the Greek priest in the community. This was an unrelenting issue that would be brought up at almost every social function. I wondered if there was a priest anywhere who could make the entire Greek community happy. I remember my aunt Tony, Uncle Chris's wife, a stunning woman of slight stature and mild demeanor, with shiny, short black hair and an apron around her waist, working tirelessly in the kitchen to continue to provide μεζεδαικια, καφε, and ποτη (hors d'oeuvres, coffee, and alcoholic drinks) to the guests. I always thought, if she were clothed in an Athenian white robe, she could have been the prototypical Greek goddess.

And the festive pilgrimage continued! Beginning with my aunt Harriet's home for Thanksgiving, moving to my uncle Chris's home for Christmas, and returning to my aunt Harriet's home for New Year's. It was as if we were a group of Greek nomads.

New Year's Day (Βασιλοπιτα) is another significant day for the Greeks and is the name day for anyone named Basil, after Saint Basil the Great, Greek Archbishop of Caesarea, also known as the "revealer of heavenly mysteries," "a renowned and bright star," and "the glory and beauty of the Church." The same family members would congregate at my uncle Bill's home to celebrate his name day.

I remember, as children, we would kneel before my uncle, and he would give us a few silver coins. My aunt would make the spanakopita and deposit a silver quarter somewhere in the dough. It is Greek tradition that either the spanakopita or the Saint Basil bread has a silver coin baked into it, and whoever receives the slice with the coin will receive the blessing of Saint Basil for the coming year. I still have olfactory memories of that pita as it was baking in the oven. When it was ready, she would cut it into several pieces, and the person whose piece contained the quarter would have good luck for the new year. Although I wasn't aware of it at that time, my aunt would slip a coin into each child's piece.

Funerals

Within the Greek community, funerals remain multiday social events. Whenever I spoke with my mother by telephone, I could immediately sense when someone in the Greek community had died, by the pitch of her voice and the rapid cadence of her speech. Without question, when a funeral was upcoming, there was a distinct excitement in her voice that was absent during her normal conversation. After all, as with any social event, substantial preparations had to commence at an accelerated pace. Food had to be prepared, mourners contacted, and lamentations begun. In those days, wakes were significant social events, and in many cases, the parlor, in the tenement rather than the funeral home, was utilized and had to be organized. That was the case when my grandfather died.

Since my grandfather lived on the third floor, my uncles were confronted with a grueling and challenging mission. And that was to precariously hoist his casket on their shoulders and carry it unsteadily upstairs to the third-floor apartment via a tortuous, narrow, poorly lit wooden staircase that turned sharply at each landing. Changing positions erratically and unsteadily throughout the slow laborious ascent, these attendants, bolstered by alcohol to compensate for oxygen deprivation, finally reached the summit and positioned the casket on a large wooden table in the parlor, surrounded by candles that remained continuously lit and, for the most part, unattended. For that reason, I always thought it was the will of the gods that the tenement did not burn down.

Throughout the waking period, various types of food and pastries were available to those paying their respects, and ouzo and tsipouro were available as well but, of course, only for medicinal and sedative purposes. Finally, when the wake had concluded, the casket was perilously carried down the same narrow stairwell by my ouzo-fortified uncles, and after frequent contacts with the sides of the wall, as well as the railing, during the descent, it was carefully placed in a hearse and delivered to the church for the funeral.

In accordance with Greek tradition, the casket remained open and faced east during the funeral service.

Typical at Greek wakes, and I'm sure this can be validated for other ethnicities as well, after an inauspicious period of tranquility, a group of older women dressed in their customary black mourning outfits would arrive almost as if choreographed and on cue, sobbing at the outset, and quickly escalating to cries that would rapidly agitate the women who were otherwise sitting reserved. In a matter of minutes, the room would transform into a crescendo of moans, cries, and shrieks. After witnessing this performance at several wakes, I joked about organizing a group of professional mourners that could be rented for these occasions.

It is tradition and typical for older Greek women who have lost their husbands or another family member to wear black for at least one year after a death, and it is not unusual for older generations of Greek women to wear black mourning clothes that include dress, scarf, nylons, and shoes for the remainder of their lives, even though this practice appears to be declining with subsequent generations.

Following my father's death, my mother continued to wear either black or dark-colored clothes for the remainder of her life. The term μελαννειμονεω means "I dress in black." Men, in contrast, generally wear black armbands (ζωνες μαυρου βραχιονα) for forty days following a death. The significance of the forty days is that it represents the time when the soul is judged. It is Orthodox tradition that, at the end of forty days and at the end of the first year, memorial masses for the deceased are celebrated.

Regardless of the seriousness of any occasion, at least with the Greeks, inevitably there are always upbeat moments that briefly ease the sadness. In addition, with Greeks, you can always expect the unexpected. There were a few of these moments at my mother's wake and funeral. It seems that at any wake, at some point, the conversation unavoidably turns to include other deceased members of the family. It was no different at my mother's wake, and it came at a time when my wife and I were sitting with my cousins and my aunt Kelly, my mother's youngest and most chaotic and volatile sister, who had now assumed the matriarchal role in the family. Suddenly, as if she were struck by a bolt of lightning from Olympus, she began to describe in animated terms the shocking details involving blister boy. *Blister boy?* I thought. *Who is she talking about?*

I sat stunned and astonished, not knowing who blister boy was and what his significance was at my mother's wake. My aunt Kelly informed us in graphic detail in her frenzied way that blister boy was their brother who had died when he was a child from a blister on his foot that became infected, attributed to poorly fitting shoes. Until that moment, I never knew who blister boy was, and my aunt Kelly was elated that she had provided us with previously unknown details regarding our family tree.

But it didn't end there. The saga of blister boy continued the next day. Prior to the funeral, as the limousine with our family inside was entering the cemetery, the tranquility was abruptly shattered when suddenly my younger cousin Johanna, who you would never know was present because she was otherwise so quiet, unexpectedly and completely out of character blurted out, "Over there! That is where blister boy is buried!" Completely flabbergasted that she spoke at all, and further that she spoke with such conviction, we laughed hysterically! Tragic as the blister boy incident must have been for my mother's family, at this moment, the sincerity of Johanna's exclamation, combined with the sudden animated expression on her otherwise submissive demeanor, provided a moment of welcome laughter.

Later, just as the graveside service for my mother was concluding and we were preparing to leave the cemetery, a car turned around the corner and came to an abrupt and unexpected stop. Within seconds, a lady sprang out, holding a camera in one hand and gesturing wildly with her free arm. At this point, none of us knew what to think as she approached our family. Speaking excitedly in English with a heavy Greek accent, this mysterious lady politely but firmly directed the family to line up. Admittedly, I was completely perplexed, and I failed to ask her who she was or why she was there, but before I knew it, we were obediently lining up on the rough terrain, which was quite a feat for those in heels. She then took several photographs of the family.

Shortly thereafter, the mystery was solved. She advised us that she was from the same region in Greece where our family was from, and she wanted to send back photographs of the family. Even though I found it rather bizarre at that time, when I thought about it later, it was an engaging gesture and represented a sincere attempt to communicate with relatives and friends in Greece, which represents another example of how extensive the Greek extended family can be. Considered from an alternative perspective, it confirms that the Greek funeral is a social event!

WHILE I WAS GROWING UP, it seemed like the Greeks had more holidays than anyone else. And on these occasions, of course, I was expected to be present with my parents. During these events, I would rather have been with my friends, but I quickly realized that, assuredly, they were also with their families celebrating the same holiday. But I eventually understood that holidays, in addition to their religious and cultural significance, provided a mechanism by which the extended family remained intact, ethnic values and cultural traditions were preserved, and Greekness was protected.

CONCLUSION

Assimilation and My Greek Legacy

"The years fall, as do the swallows"
Πεφτανε τα χρονια σαν τα χελιδονια

ALTHOUGH I WASN'T AWARE OF it at the time, the assimilation process began before I left the agora in which I grew up. It began the moment I left the Greek section for the first time and went to college. Prior to this, almost everything I did, and most of my experiences, were confined to the agora and involved Greeks. When I was accepted to Boston University in the spring of my senior year in high school, I was given a sweatshirt with Boston University on the front. But at that time, nothing had changed. However, once fall arrived, and I traveled to Boston, the umbrella of security that the agora had provided suddenly disappeared, and I became exposed to other cultures and ethnicities. The assimilation process began, and things would never be the same.

I suddenly found myself at Boston University living on the ninth floor of a hotel converted into a dormitory that housed approximately one thousand students, none of whom I knew. Even worse, no one that I knew was attending Boston University; most of my friends were enrolled at the University of New Hampshire. I have a keen recollection of the intense loneliness I felt during that first semester and that distressing period; not a day passed that I didn't want to leave Boston and return to the more familiar agora.

My feelings of loneliness became so intense that I came home every weekend and on days when I didn't have classes. I came home for a few hours in the evening to play in a basketball league at the YMCA and to be with other Greek friends. The ethnic magnet became so powerful that I would walk by the Greek cathedral in Boston several times a week, which would provide temporary reassurance. The security of the agora was so formidable that it took me at least a year to become even remotely comfortable in my new environment.

Most likely due to my strong cultural background, and partly because of my reluctance to interact in such a foreign environment, I maintained a dominant sense of Greekness that included the strong Hellenic values instilled into me as a child. Also of significance, I am sure, were my mother's persistent warnings, "Don't trust non-Greek strangers; they are not like us!" Although I never asked her, this advice was probably given to her by her parents as well. Even though she meant well, these words only reinforced my anxiety.

I developed some relief from my anxiety by examining the weekly regional Greek newspaper, not only for its local news but also for its social events column that enabled me to locate the next Church-sponsored Greek dance in the area. I would coerce my non-Greek roommates to come with me, and I laughed as they stumbled through the dance steps. Moreover, a significant comforting factor, as well as a positive element in my cultural adaptation, was that my childhood friend Chris was only a short subway ride away at Tufts University, across the Charles River in Medford, Massachusetts. Although I never confronted him about my feelings, I am willing to bet that he experienced them also. We visited each other several times a week during the fall and winter seasons, and we came back to the agora together on weekends.

ASSIMILATION AND MY GREEK LEGACY

Finally, spring came, and with it, my greatest love at the time, baseball. I was on the team at Boston University, and gradually, the city didn't seem to be such a bad place after all. The process was apparently succeeding, and I began to acclimate, develop more confidence, and for the first time, gradually began to become a Bostonian. Insidiously but purposefully, the city began to attract me as if I were being drawn into the valley of the Sirens. While at the same time, even though I was unaware of it, the simplicity of the agora began to loosen its grip on me as I became increasingly more fascinated with the multidimensional complexity of the city.

When I graduated, I became a part-time faculty member and graduate student, and the dean of the college asked me to tutor an undergraduate student in physiology. At the same time, he assigned us both to a project that involved the rehabilitation of a disabled child within the Greater Boston area. That undergraduate student eventually became my wife. Pam and I were married in both Roman Catholic and Greek Orthodox Churches with a traditional Greek ceremony followed by a reception that included both Greek and American music. We both continue to respect our heritage, and she has always encouraged me to retain my Greek traditions. She has been the catalyst and my greatest supporter as I endeavor to complete this story.

Having spent most of my time as a Bostonian and preparing to become a Connecticut Yankee, I failed to realize that the agora in New Hampshire was undergoing a transition. When I finally recognized it, that transition appeared to be abrupt and extensive. While I was in Boston, the agora as I knew it had all but disappeared. Yes, there was a coffeehouse here, a Greek market there, but in between was a multistory housing development and a civic center. The definable agora had disappeared, making it extremely difficult to find the Greeks. Times have changed over the years, and the Greek community that I grew up in and loved has since transformed and virtually disappeared. Unfortunately, this appears to be typical of most Greek agoras.

Greeks have dispersed as they have become integrated into society in general, leaving only remnants of the typical agoras. Despite this change, as Greeks, we strive to maintain our Greek heritage and cultural values and impart our sense of Greekness to our children so they understand what it is like to be a Greek American. Furthermore, we are notorious for displaying a nostalgia for what is lost. Talk to a middle-aged or older Greek, and they will quickly reminisce about the old days when there was more cohesion and less assimilation, when Greeks were more likely to be found in Greek sections where they congregated in the taverna, the agora, or the church.

Currently, Greeks, as well as many other ethnicities, have been separated from their agoras as urbanization increases and assimilation progresses, and this greatly enhances the probability that traditions will become further jeopardized. From my perspective, cultural erosion has expanded, and we have lost some aspects of our sense of Greekness. It is most unfortunate, since the fabric of this country has been woven by immigrants withdrawing into their subcultures after the workday to maintain ethnic stability within their families and their community.

Nevertheless, despite the increasing tendency toward assimilation, many older Greeks continue to defy acculturation, even though in many communities only isolated pockets of the agora remain. Coffeehouses, although struggling to persist, remain viable, and Greek restaurants flourish in many communities and continue to function as sanctuaries from the difficulties of daily life, providing us with the opportunity to be with Greeks. The nearby J&G Restaurant, with its Greek specialties and its outdoor plaka, provides a hospitable atmosphere and is a popular site for Greeks, as are various other Greek restaurants in the area. I still laugh when I think of the Greek restaurateurs who, while listening to a complaint, will continue to smile and say in Greek, "We were writing philosophy while you were still swinging from the trees." ("Γραφαμε φιλοσοφια, ενω ακομα σας ηταν αιωρητας απο τα δεντρα.")

If you are in a coffeehouse and look hard enough, you will undoubtedly locate an old Greek man sitting quietly alone at a corner table with an expressionless face and a vacant stare, drinking his demitasse coffee while nervously twirling his komboloi. I can guarantee you that if you sit with him and begin talking, he will suddenly become animated and enthusiastically describe his earlier life in the agora and in Greece.

The New Agora

I accepted a teaching-research position at the University of Connecticut that gave me the opportunity to practice rehabilitation medicine, and I became a Connecticut Yankee. I imagine, because of my naivety, I became perplexed when I realized that when you relocate to a new agora, you cannot expect to develop and enjoy the same relationships you had when you were growing up. Integration within a new Greek agora was going to be more difficult than I had imagined, and despite being a Greek, initially, at least, I felt like an outsider (ξενος). As difficult as it was for me to understand, it became apparent that a Greek from Thessaloniki is different than one from Athens, or than a Greek from the Peloponnese. Even though a Greek is a Greek, in certain respects, regional differences persist.

From the outset, I didn't know any Greeks in the area. Obviously acutely aware of this dilemma, the Greek gods directed me to the local YMCA, where, in the locker room, I saw a name on a locker that ended in *os* and was so long that it needed an extension on the nameplate. That was when I met Greg P., a former marine and a practicing social worker who came from a family of Greek priests. His father and brother were priests, and after one year in the seminary, Greg had decided the profession wasn't for him. As well as being the most compassionate person I have ever met, he was filled with the Greek spirit, and he became my conduit into the new agora. As an example, for Greek Independence Day, we wanted to celebrate our heritage with an authentic Greek dinner, and with the assistance of one of his Greek friends, we were permitted entry into the Hartford Hellenic Cultural Center (known by most Greeks as the Greek club) for dinner. That night, we became members, and my attitude changed.

Greg P. was very logical, even methodical, and remained calm in all circumstances, but he could be mischievous. Everyone who knew us confirmed that he balanced my chaotic personality. I consider him to be the brother I never had. He introduced me to his Greek friends in the area and, among them, to his very close friend, another Greg, who many years ago left New Hampshire after college to relocate to Florida. While on his trip, he stopped in Hartford to visit friends, met a local Greek woman, and never left. They subsequently married and remained in Hartford. As if the gods had commanded, it was the same Greg C. who had lived in Keene, New Hampshire and who threw rolled-up pieces of paper into the light fixtures with me at my aunt Harriet's home in Manchester, New Hampshire, when I was a child! I was flabbergasted and considered it more than a remarkable coincidence! I remain convinced that this was a deliberate directive from Zeus that I be united once again with a Greek from the old agora. Although he fought like the marine that he was, Greg P. succumbed to cancer when he was fifty-nine years old. It was devastating for me to have lost my Greek warrior brother. I will never forget him.

One of the remnants of the agora in my community is the Hartford Hellenic Cultural Center, formerly known as the Hartford Hellenic Soccer Club, and known by many as the Greek club. The Greek club is tucked into a corner within the multiethnic section of the historic south end of Hartford and occupies an inconspicuous yellow, one-story cement building protected on two sides by small parking lots. Any hint of its character may be gleaned from Greek and American flags, positioned above a front patio, that are vaguely symbolic of Evzones guarding the Tomb of the Unknown Soldier at Syntagma. The patio, known as the plaka by its members, is enclosed by a three-foot-high faded black wrought-iron fence, within which are several faded, umbrella-topped, weather-beaten tables that provide a taverna-like atmosphere for all aspects of outdoor Greek life, including "conspiratorial activity."

The Greek club remains a popular focus for Greeks as they look for their own. It provides me with the opportunity to read the Greek newspapers, watch the news from Greece, speak Greek with my friends, and enjoy traditional Greek food. I am proud that I am fluent in all aspects of the language, and to ensure I will remain that way, I make regular visits to the local kafenion, where I can speak to other Greeks, read the Greek newspapers, watch the Greek cable television stations, and of course, argue about sports and politics. And the Greek salad (χωριατικι σαλατα), porgy (τσιπουρα), and lemon potatoes (πατατες λεμονιου) aren't too bad, either!

I have taken many of my non-Greek friends to the Greek club for a typical Greek meal and a Hellenic cultural experience, and it is always fascinating to observe the dynamics as they evolve after we arrive. Understandably, from a non-Greek's perspective, appearance at the Greek club can be quite an intimidating experience, comparable to suddenly finding yourself dropped into a kafenion in Athens without an escort or a translator; it's an alien environment, to say the least. Although this may be the initial reaction at the Hellenic Cultural Center, it is brief, rapidly replaced by the attainment of kefi.

Two locked, windowless side doors, with a sign declaring MEMBERS ONLY, opened only by a member's key, immediately catapulted us back in time to a place remarkably comparable to an Athens kafenion in the 1950s. Our immediate sensation was olfactory, as my friends detected and hungrily described a variety of unknown but tantalizingly appetizing aromas. For me, images of bouzoukia and dance (μπουζουκια και χορος) at Sissifos Taverna in the Plaka section of Athens and eating spanakopita as a child in Aunt Mary's home in Manchester, New Hampshire flashed through my mind.

Abruptly, however, we were transported to the present day as we were confronted by several sets of suspicious eyes, which shifted their attention from card games, the television, or from the daily Greek newspaper to warily stare and scrutinize us. After a few seconds, my friends cautiously scanned the room and noticed clusters of Greeks gesturing, flailing their arms, and speaking loudly in a foreign language. To their relief, they were quickly informed that the members were arguing with one another about recent soccer results or current political events. Following this brief period, that seemed like an eternity, of innocuous scrutiny by a few of the older evzones, we were eventually welcomed and acknowledged with the traditional greeting. The graciousness extended to my friends by the Greek members is a characteristic example of filoxenia.

Alekos, the chef, cordially greeted us with the traditional για σου, which is an expression of welcome and good health, and we sat at a checkered vinyl, cloth-covered table close to a large flat-screen television precariously balancing on a wobbly stand and broadcasting the daily news from Greece at a deafening volume. Even though no one appeared to be watching, except for an isolated member in the corner, who was nervously manipulating his worry beads (κομπολοι), I wasn't courageous enough to suggest that the channel be changed or that the volume be lowered.

Feeling much less conspicuous and more comfortable now that we were seated, my non-Greek friends noticed several septuagenarians, octogenarians, and a few nonagenarians among the members. Moreover, they were astonished that these old men were so energetic, since disability is a serious problem that threatens the independence of so many elder members of our society. I laughed and explained that it may be attributed, in part at least, to their cultural lifestyle that includes the Mediterranean diet.

The main room in the Hellenic Cultural Center consists of several tables neatly arranged around the periphery under windows that, when not covered by venetian blinds, looked out at the plaka, in addition to several tables haphazardly placed within the room. To our immediate left, a refrigerated cooler containing bottled water, soft drinks, and fruit separated us from an incredibly small but immaculate kitchen, adequately equipped with a refrigerator and a stainless-steel sink, highlighted by a massive black iron gas stove with all four burners flaming like the Olympic torch. Hunched over this fiery caldera, as if appealing for guidance from the Oracle of Delphi, or observing Atlantis vanish beneath the Mediterranean, effectively managing a cluster of steaming pots was Alekos (Αλεκος), the host, cook, waiter, cashier, and dishwasher, all in one. My friends were amazed that this man single-handedly completed the tasks that conventionally required an entire staff. Incidentally, I forgot to mention that Αλεκος is an octogenarian!

ASSIMILATION AND MY GREEK LEGACY

One of the benefits of membership at the Hellenic Cultural Center is that Alekos previously owned and operated a local Greek restaurant and has the mysterious ability to provide delicious dinners despite the rudimentary kitchen within which he operates. There are no menus here, and Alekos simply informed us of the items available, which included various types of meat and fish. He proudly invited us to inspect the kitchen, and to select the fish or piece of meat of our choice, another Greek tradition.

Within a few minutes, the atmosphere changed when, in a traditional gesture of filoxenia, friends began to congregate at our table, bringing wine and ouzo as well as Greek music, courtesy of cell phones. Rather quickly, following several toasts of γεια μας (life to us) in English with a Greek accent, the Greeks and their therapeutic regimen achieved their goal! Abruptly, the point of no return was quickly surpassed, and everyone became relaxed. As the Greeks exclaim, kefi had been achieved, and initial wary stares were converted to smiles and laughter. Good wine, good food, great friends, and an evening of relaxation and enjoyment—this is hospitality the Greek way! As a testimony to filoxenia, my non-Greek friends have expressed amazement as to how well they were welcomed, and in the next breath they ask, "When can we come again?"

On more than one occasion, filoxenia (φιλοξενια, hospitality) extended so far into the night that the chef apologized and said he was going home; he politely asked us to lock up when we were through celebrating. Opa! Incidentally, I have an Italian colleague who routinely drives ninety miles from his home in Rhode Island to enjoy kefi and filoxenia at the Hellenic Cultural Center. The list of non-Greeks who want to return to the Greek club continues to increase. It might have something to do with its ambiance, but I suspect it's more to do with Alekos's gastronomic proficiency.

One evening, when my friend Greg's brother Dean, a Greek priest, was in Hartford, I invited him to the Hellenic Cultural Center for dinner. As Greeks, we are taught at a young age to be respectful of elders and priests, and as soon as we arrived, the atmosphere within the Center changed noticeably.

Suddenly, all activities came to a standstill, and that included card games, a beloved Greek activity. Moreover, the volume on the television was lowered to an inaudible level, the typical raucous conversation abruptly became subdued, and facial countenances went from relaxed to inexpressive. And with good reason, because "a priest had arrived" ("ο ιερεας ειχε φτασει")!

And why was he here? Did someone die? To dispel their fears, however, within a few minutes we sat at a table and ordered a glass of wine, and everyone became relieved. Their comfort level increased even further when Father Dean informed them that he had been a bouncer in a nightclub prior to entering the seminary. After dinner, as the discussion became more spirited, we listened to Greek music on our cell phones when, unexpectedly, from an adjacent table, two old Greek men sprung up and started dancing the zeibekiko. Opa!

We Greeks are proud of our culture, and we remain united by our traditions that include wine, dance, music, and good food. Some may argue that the center of Greekness is the dinner table, where the entire family and friends gather to enjoy a meal and to discuss politics and sports. Inasmuch as the dinner table is the center of Greek culture at home, the kafenion remains a traditional part of Greek life, where men congregate in the evening to have a meal, play cards, backgammon, tavli, discuss politics or sports, or perhaps just enjoy a demitasse coffee, frappe, or ouzo.

For me, the kafenion is a valuable resource that allows me to maintain my Greek conversational skills, read the Greek newspapers, and be with other Greeks. And, of course, I enjoy the Greek cuisine as well! It continues to intrigue me that a Greek, who generally has a reputation for driving fast, will drive furiously to get to a kafenion, only to sit there in stillness sipping a frappe and twirling his komboloi for hours. I guess that's just part of being Greek.

The Greek Legacy

On a hazy moonlit evening, a little boy stood in front of the large, hazy coffeehouse (καφενιον) window trying to recognize his father inside, but he could only see indistinguishable silhouettes in the dim light. After several seconds and persistent squinting, he was finally able to see an old man sitting at a table in front of the window twirling his komboloi, his eyes seemingly searching into the emptiness. Excitedly, that little boy smiled and waved at him, but before the old man recognized him and could wave back, the little boy, barely visible through the hazy window, faded gently into the night.

Suddenly, as if Zeus had charged me with a lightning bolt, I grasped the implication of my vision, and I was staggered by the realization that the image of that little boy outside the window was my reflection. It was me, standing in front of that coffeehouse window many years ago, searching for my father. Astounded and deprived by the lack of any forewarning, I had abruptly become transformed into that old man sitting at the table by the window, twirling his komboloi.

Instantaneously, I began to appreciate what that old man was thinking many years ago. What appeared at first glance to be a vacant stare, instead represented a profound, personal, and intimate reflection of my life. It seems like only a fraction of a second has passed since I was peering through that coffeehouse window looking for my father, but suddenly I have taken his place. As the Greeks say, the years fall, as do the swallows (πεφτανε τα χρονια σαν τα χελιδονια).

I have progressed through the cycle from son to father and now to grandfather (παπου), and I consider myself, as I am sure you do also, to be the most fortunate Greek on earth. Before I realized it, while my daughter, Samantha, was in her final year in college, she came to me and said, "Dad, I met the person I want to marry!" She brought Peter home, and I told her that I could not have chosen anyone more appropriate for her. As parents, we realized that one day our children would grow up to be young adults and eventually marry, and that day had arrived. We spent several months planning the wonderful event, and finally my daughter's wedding day was here. Despite the chaos associated with such a celebration, I was bombarded by myriad emotions, and it was a surreal experience.

As all brides are, my beautiful daughter was radiant as we smiled, walking down the aisle to the traditional wedding song. As we approached the altar, I perceived numerous inexpressible emotions, and I knew things would never be the same for me again. I held her hand securely, and when we finally approached her groom, I carefully pulled back her veil, kissed her gently on each cheek, as is Greek tradition, and then placed her hand securely into Peter's waiting open hand. With that gesture, I gave my daughter to him, to love and to protect her. This was an extremely impactful moment for me, since there is a special bond between a father and daughter.

At the reception, we danced to the song "Turn Around," and so many memories flashed through my mind. As all fathers do, I could not believe that my daughter had grown up so quickly to become a beautiful young woman and, eventually, the mother of my marvelous grandchildren (εγγονια). Yes, indeed she has! But to me, she is still and will always be my little girl.

And then, there is the event that all Greeks anticipate. As the electrocardiogram continued to assure us by its steady signal on the monitor, there they were, two tiny little independent hearts beating anxiously within their mother's abdomen, each impatiently waiting to arrive, to make their presence known, and of course, to create further chaos (χαος) in our lives. And then suddenly, the moment was here, and they came to us. I caught a glimpse of them as they were taken to the neonatal intensive care unit (NICU) from the delivery room, my grandson breathing more easily with the assistance of a C-PAP unit, and my granddaughter staring into the corridor looking for her family. Later that evening, as I held them securely while rocking them in the NICU, I realized the significance of the miracle and my responsibility as a grandfather. God has given us two of his tiny angels and has imparted to me a greater purpose in life.

Grandchildren are what every Greek man lives for! I am a proud grandfather, a παπου, and I thank God for blessing our family with twin grandchildren. Please meet Gabriel, my brown-eyed Spartan warrior, and Alexsandria, my little blue-eyed goddess from Delphi. Their eyes twinkle like the stars in

ASSIMILATION AND MY GREEK LEGACY

the Aegean night! (Και τα ματια τους λυγιζουν σαν τα αστερια στη νυχτα του Αιγαιου!) As Greeks, you can appreciate that they have become my life! A few years ago, while we were playing, I asked them where they came from, and without hesitation and quite convincingly, they replied, "God sent us." I simply smiled.

Although I can't play baseball any longer, my grandson uses my glove, and that is the greatest honor he could give to me. When he puts his hand into that glove, I am playing again. A few days ago, despite some knee discomfort that I know he sensed but that I certainly wasn't going to admit, I struggled to get into a catcher's position and throw the ball with him. I smiled as I attempted to catch his fastball. In him, I saw myself many years earlier. Frequently before bedtime, my grandchildren will sit on my lap or cuddle on either side of me in bed and remain captivated when I describe fables about Greek mythology. Alex generally falls asleep first, following an exhausting day at Delphi, while Gabe becomes more alert and is prepared to take his shield and join King Leonidas and the "300" in the defense at Thermopolae. I thank God every day for giving me my two precious gifts!

I have a wonderful family in excellent health (ηγεια), and as Alexis Zorba would say, the "full catastrophe" ("την πληρη καταστροφη"). I could have done things differently as I progressed through life, but I believe this was the path that was chosen for me. It is as if destiny was guiding this journey. I remain convinced that it could not have been any different, because I would not have been blessed with Pamela, Samantha, Peter, Alexsandria, and Gabriel. Given the opportunity to do it over again, I would not change anything, because my family has made my life a dream come true.

Occasionally, I wish I could go back to those earlier, less complicated times when we were together in the agora, but the gods have a way of controlling the direction of the winds of life. Now that we have become dispersed and assimilated to some extent, things are more challenging, but nonetheless we continue to preserve our traditions and our heritage. Our needs became our children's needs and then our grandchildren's needs. Our wants have become secondary to us, but we accept that willingly, because that is the Greek way.

Growing old is not a curse but indeed a precious gift, because it provides us with the opportunity to see our families, our children, our grandchildren, and maybe even our great-grandchildren develop. Many years ago, I pierced my daughter's ears in preparation for earrings, and last night I pierced my eight-year-old granddaughter's ears as well. Having completed the procedure, I could see that her eyes welled up with tears from the discomfort, but she remained brave. After a few minutes, and while she remained unaware, I glanced at her as she was examining her new earrings in the mirror. Apparently satisfied with the results, she smiled as she came to me, hugged me, and said, "Thank you, παπου! When I have a daughter, I'm going to have you pierce her ears too." I smiled, nodded in agreement, and thought how innocent and endearing that statement was. Indeed, it was a portrayal of the marvelous innocence of that age. And most important, *Whenever she looks in the mirror, she will remember her παπου*!

Furthermore, she may even seize a reflection of her παπου winking at her. And who knows? If the gods are willing, I will pierce my great-granddaughter's ears as well. Always remember that time is the most precious commodity. Use it wisely; love your family.

We all eventually reach a point in our lives where we become responsible for all the lives that we touch. The circle has almost become complete. But before it closes, I will continue to provide for my family to the best of my ability, because, after all, it's the Greek way. As Pericles eloquently said, "What you leave behind is not what is engraved in stone monuments but what is woven into the lives of others." Even though I am closer to the end than to the beginning, as a Greek, I prefer to look at it from Zorba's perspective when he proclaimed, "Life is trouble, only death is not. To be alive is to undo your belt and look for trouble!"[6] And as Leonidas, the general of the

---

6   Nicholas Kazantzakis, *Zorba the Greek* (New York: Simon & Schuster, 1952).

ASSIMILATION AND MY GREEK LEGACY

300 Spartans at Thermopolae defiantly exclaimed, "Μολων Λαβε!" "Come and get it!" One final thought: Even though the circle is almost complete, no one is certain that it cannot make another revolution, because, after all, we are Greeks, aren't we?

Today is New Year's Day, and I'm watching a football game and thinking about the times when I was younger and at my aunt's home with my Greek family enjoying the holiday, Greek style.

And so, my friends, it is time for me to stop writing, because my grandchildren will be here soon, excitedly searching for the quarter in their pieces of spanakopita, so I must be certain that they choose the right pieces. In addition, I must shine two silver dollars for their good fortune.

In conclusion, I hope I have provided you with some laughter and with several unforgettable memories of what it was like to be brought up as Greek Americans in my generation. Without a doubt, it was a unique time that will never be replicated. I have enjoyed writing this account of "our generation," and I hope you enjoyed reading it. Yassou, and be well! (Γεια Σας, και να ειστε καλα!) And foremost, don't forget "to close your eyes and remember everything good!"

To my Greek readers, I hope I have rekindled some memories. And to my non-Greek readers, I hope I have given you a glimpse into the Greek culture and catalyzed similar memories of events that you may have experienced. And to all my readers, both Greek and non-Greek, I hope you have found my book entertaining, that I made you laugh, and that I reminded you that we are all a lot more alike than we are different.

EPILOGUE

It Is the Will of the Gods: I'm Coming Home, Dad

WHILE MY FATHER WAS STILL alive, I promised him that I would go to Greece so that I could understand where he came from. And I did, on several occasions. Most Greek Americans express a desire to travel to Greece to see where their parents came from. I am convinced that, since I took my first breath, the gods willed this odyssey. Since my ancestral beginnings, my spirit (πνευμα) was there, and the gods were commanding me to return to it. But to attempt to describe this emotion is challenging. It is an intangible element, an undefinable sense, an obsession, often subliminal but always present, and possibly emanating from the soul (Ψυχη). It is greater than a restlessness; it's more like a compulsion that had to be fulfilled, a requirement to return to where it all began. It must be part of this sense of "Greekness" that includes passion, chaos, the love of life, and filotimo. My story could not be completed until I took this odyssey. "I'm coming home, Dad!"

Getting There

The most interesting flight experience I have ever had was on my first trip to Greece. Prior to my departure, I was forewarned about flying to Greece in an airplane filled with Greeks, but the details of what I should expect were purposely excluded. When my departure date arrived and I got to JFK airport in New York City, I discovered why the particulars were omitted.

As scores of Greeks began to arrive and assemble at the departure gate, the tranquility was shattered, and that section at JFK airport was transformed into an agora-like atmosphere with a perceptible escalation in both commotion and volume. It began with a distinct, yet reasonable, hum that eventually became a loud clamor as the level of restlessness markedly increased.

Greek women in their traditional mourning outfits began to form groups and talk excitedly, while men paced impatiently, some nervously manipulating their komboloi. Others appeared to be wandering silently and without purpose within the departure area, even though the departure time for Athens was four hours away. Without hesitation, brown paper bags were opened, and spanakopita was offered. The waiting area resembled a Greek festival.

Eventually, having completed a laborious check-in process that included seat assignment and baggage check-in, several passengers assembled at the entry door to the Jetway at least forty-five minutes prior to departure. Since the gate attendant quickly became bewildered, I assumed that this was her first assignment with Greek voyagers.

By Greek standards, the line was reasonably orderly, at least initially, but as the departure time approached, it developed into an undulating wave that suddenly erupted into a frenetic sprint to the aircraft when the entry door to the Jetway finally opened. This prompted me to think of mythology when Jason and his Argonauts set their eyes on the Golden Fleece, which in this instance was the aircraft preparing to transport us to Athens. Here, it was two hundred restless Greek Argonauts stampeding through the Jetway past the stunned flight attendant at the plane's entry door. And that's not all. Imagine this scenario and, further, what the flight attendants had to deal with. Two hundred Greeks finally in the plane, many of them claiming that they had the same seat. It did not make any difference to them that the seats were preassigned.

Eventually, after that calamity was resolved and everyone was sitting, at least for the moment, the plane began to taxi down the runway and all appeared to be well, but I could sense a feeling of uneasiness developing among most of the passengers. And then abruptly, as if on cue, as the plane began its takeoff, most of the Argonauts began to make the sign of the cross.

When we finally reached altitude and the pilot announced that we could unfasten our seat belts, it seemed that most of the Argonauts made a simultaneous dash for the restrooms. Eventually, assisted by wine from the gods, most of them settled down, and the flight was uneventful until the plane landed. At that point, everyone again made the sign of the cross, then began applauding the pilot enthusiastically and congratulating him loudly for a safe voyage—an ideal example of Greek anxiety followed by Greek enthusiasm!

Arriving

Having landed at the airport in midmorning on my first trip to Greece and after grabbing a frappe, I secured a cab and headed for Athens. The old airport, prior to the Olympic games, was in Glyfada, a suburb of Athens. As we proceeded through Glyfada, on Poseidon Avenue (Λεωφορο Ποσειδον), on the left I could see the beautiful tranquil blue waters of the Saronic Gulf glistening in the bright sunlight as the waves crested and danced mischievously, mimicking Poseidon's nymphs. On the opposite side of the cab beyond the shops, the barren sun-bleached hills became apparent, and I visualized Leonidas and his Spartan warriors advancing toward us. We passed Saint Kosmas Marina (named for Saint Kosmas of Aetolia, and unfortunately not for me), continued to Apollonos Avenue (Λεωφορος Απολλωνος), and to Zefirou Avenue (Λεωφορος Ζεφυρου).

Abruptly, the cab took a right turn and proceeded on to L. Andrea

Siggrou (Λεωφορειο Συγγρου). Suddenly, there it was! I had read about it, seen pictures, posters, and paintings of it. And now my eyes became transfixed on it. It was breathtaking and, in my opinion, the most magnificent structure that a Greek could see. Its majesty immediately sent chills through my spine, quickly filled me with intense warmth, and brought tears to my eyes. I was overcome with an unimaginable pride regarding my heritage. Flashes of my parents and grandparents rapidly infiltrated into and swept through my brain. I was here. I was home. I had come back to my homeland! (επεστρεψα στην πατριδα μου!) Majestically standing there, rising above Athens on the Acropolis, its Doric white marble shining radiantly in the midmorning sunlight against a sparkling Grecian blue sky, was the Parthenon, standing guard over Athens like an Evzone. I will never forget that sight! "I'm home, Dad!"

Plaka

On one of the highest sections within the ancient city of Athens, the Plaka section of Athens, and remote from the tourist area, sits a small, tree-enclosed, innocuous taverna adjacent to the wall of the Acropolis close to Saint George Church on Strattonos (Στρατωνος) that provides a spectacular view of the Parthenon. It is run by Haralambros, Harry, a sixty-year-old Greek and his eighty-year-old mother. A persistent smoker and constant talker, Harry is repeatedly pursued by his mother to either cook or to remove dishes from the tables.

I got to know Harry, since I frequented that taverna daily while I was in Athens. We would sit under the cooling effect of the trees during the hot Athenian afternoons and discuss the state of the world while drinking wine and eating salad, only to return later that evening for dinner. I frequently think of Harry and that taverna and how uncomplicated life is under certain circumstances. From any table in that taverna, patrons can see the Greek flag flying proudly over the Acropolis against the blue Aegean sky, advising tourists that they are within the cradle of democracy and reminding Greeks of their proud heritage. The Greek flag is comprised of nine blue and nine white horizontal stripes that stand for the syllables of the Greek motto "Eleftheria i Thanatos" ("Ελευθερια η θανατος"), freedom or death. The blue represents the sky and the sea, and the white stands for the purity of the struggle for freedom. The upper left corner is the traditional Greek Orthodox cross.

Syntagma Square: Evzones

One of the places I knew I must see was the Tomb of the Unknown Soldier in front of the Hellenic Parliament building at Syntagma Square. The tomb is under constant protection of the Evzones. They comprise a special unit of the Hellenic Army known as the Tsoliades (τσολιαδες), a name originally given to the Greek army unit that fought in the mountains, and now known as the Presidential Guard, an elite ceremonial unit that guards the Tomb of the Unknown Soldier, the presidential mansion, and the gate of the Evzone camp in Athens.

The evzone, also known as a Tsolias (τσολιας), goes back to Homer in the *Iliad* and means "well belted" in Ancient Greece. Evzones are selected from the Greek Special Forces, and to qualify, a soldier must be at least 1.87 meters (6.13 feet) tall. (Certainly, nothing like me—that scrawny little "evzone" with the oversized red clogs with black pompoms (τσαρουχια) who carried a wooden rifle onstage on Greek Independence Day.) A friend of mine from Rhodes was a former Presidential Guard, and he told me that, because of the accessories, two people are required to dress an Evzone. From this account, can you imagine how cumbersome it must be to wear the Evzone's uniform!

The changing of the guard at the Tomb of the Unknown Soldier in front of the Parliament building is an inspiring event that I considered the highlight of my first trip to Greece. As four Evzones and an escorting "Corporal of the Change" left their barracks behind the Parliament building and marched down Vasilissis Sophias Avenue (Λεωφορος Βασιλισσης Σοφιας), I still have difficulty describing my feelings, except that I felt an intense sense of Greekness as I watched them approach the Tomb of the Unknown Soldier for the hourly "little changes" of the guard. Two Evzones replaced the two sentries on duty, who returned to their barracks escorted by two Evzones and the "Corporal of the Change." The "Grand Change" occurs every Sunday morning at 11:00 a.m., when a full detachment of Evzones, dressed in their more formal, ceremonial foustanella (φουστανελας) march into the square, followed by a full detachment of regular army soldiers and the military band. Following the Greek national anthem, the exchange of the guard proceeds, and the procession returns to the barracks. An example of ethnic pride, this is an event that my daughter and grandchildren absolutely must see.

Because my grandfather was an Evzone, it has always been my aspiration to stand next to a Tsolias. And on this warm, sunny day at Syntagma, I had the opportunity. As I approached him, he appeared to become more imposing, standing motionless and at attention with an expressionless face, his eyes fixed straight ahead, a defender of the Hellenic Republic. Although I stood next to him for only a few seconds while I was being photographed by my colleague, I was mesmerized and felt an incredible sense of ethnic pride. And before I stepped away, I remember saying to him "γασσου παλικαρη," και "Ζητω Ελλας!" ("for you lad," and "long live Greece!").

It was a profoundly poignant experience, and I wonder what he thought as I stood there next to him. I hope he realized that we are proud of him as a defender of Greece. Had he been able to see my eyes, he would have understood that here was a Greek, standing with him, who also had the blood of ancient Greek warriors running through his veins. Later, while my colleague and I were sharing a bottle of wine with Haralambros at his taverna in the Plaka, he showed me the photograph. I beamed, and then I laughed. The man in the photograph was older, shorter, and with one shoulder slightly higher than the other. Despite that, and if only for a few seconds, I was an Evzone, but forever, I am a Greek.

The sculpture at the Tomb of the Unknown Soldier depicts a dead warrior lying on the ground holding a shield in his left hand and wearing an ancient battle helmet. Adjacent to the sculpture is a quote from Pericles's funeral oration of 430 BC, delivered after the first year of the Peloponnesian War to honor the fallen Athenians, as well as the names of places where Greeks have fought in the wars. The inscriptions over the Tomb of the Unknown Soldier read: to the left of the sculpture "ΜΙΑ ΚΛΙΝΗ ΚΕΝΗ ΦΕΡΕΤΑΙ ΕΣΤΡΩΜΕΝΗ ΤΩΝ ΑΦΑΝΩΝ" ("There's one empty bier made up for the unidentified [fallen] ones"); to the right "ΑΝΔΡΩΝ ΕΠΙΦΑΝΩΝ ΠΑΣΑ ΓΗ ΤΑΦΟΣ" ("The whole earth is the sepulcher of famous men."[7]). Over the sculpture in smaller writing are the words "ΕΙΣ ΑΦΑΝΗ ΣΤΡΑΤΙΩΤΗ" ("To an unknown soldier").

Lycabettus

While in Athens, one of the more spectacular views of the city, Piraeus, and the Saronic Gulf is from the top of Lycabettus (Λυκαβηττος) an 886-foot (270 meters) mountain, known as the "mountain of wolves," that rises in the center of the city. Legend has it that it was once inhabited by wolves, and I knew I had to see it.

From the center of Athens on Vasilissis Sophias Avenue (Λεωφορος βασιλισσις Σοφιας), Lycabettus is approximately twenty minutes by foot. To get to the summit, a funicular operates on a regular schedule and offers a speedy and comfortable ride. Cabs to the summit are available as well. For the Greek warriors, there is a footpath (μονοπατι), which is the path I decided to take, that begins at the end of Aristippou Street (Λεωφορειο Αριστιππου) in the Kolonaki section ("little column"; Κολωνακι), accessible by a staircase on Kleomenous Street (Λεωφορειο Κλεομενους), just before reaching the Saint George Lycabettus Hotel on the right. From this point, a sinuous path, partially shaded from the sun by olive and fir trees on either side, begins initially as a gradual ascent and becomes more demanding as the summit is approached. Taking this latter route, however, has its distinct advantages.

---

7   Thucydides, *History of the Peloponnesian War*.

When you reach the halfway point, etched into the mountain and protected by fir trees is a small taverna that affords a spectacular view of Athens below and Piraeus and the Saronic Gulf in the distance. One of my most memorable experiences of that climb was sitting under the fir trees at that taverna with a bottle of red wine, a peasant salad (χωριατικι σαλατα), olive oil, and bread, surveying the Saronic Gulf.

From the taverna, the path became more tortuous but still quite manageable. Olive trees were replaced by short firs, and eventually a weathered wooden stairway guided me to the summit, where I came upon a simple, yet beautiful, small whitewashed stucco church with a dome supporting a gold cross. The church was originally dedicated to the prophet Elias and later was renamed the Church of Saint George.

As I opened a heavy brown wooden door and entered the church, my senses suddenly expanded. Apart from the burning incense, and I am having a difficult time describing it, I immediately sensed its Greekness. Suddenly, my eyes fixated on the front right corner next to the narthex, where, surrounded by a few burning candles on either side, and sitting quietly and inauspiciously in a rickety dark brown wooden chair, was a solitary old Greek priest. He was frail, diminutive, with a salt-and-pepper beard, and his head was covered by an epanokalimavkion (επανωκαλυμμαυχιον). Spontaneously, I thought of my father, his beloved homeland, and how ecstatic he would be knowing that I was here.

Although I had the strongest impulse to kneel before that priest and hug him, perhaps because he reminded me of my father, who—I continue to miss intensely, I simply bent over in respect, lifted my head, looked directly into his eyes, and kissed the ring on his hand as he placed his other hand on my head.[8] He smiled, and in the end, I took his hand, pressed money into it for

---

8 Greeks will bow down and kiss the ring of the priest when in his presence, since he symbolizes the earthly representative of God, and therefore, as the Greeks believe, you are kissing the ring of God. I remember whenever I kissed the ring of the priest, it gave me a sense of security, and I felt I was in the presence of the protector.

the church, lit a candle, kissed the icon of the Virgin Mary, and quietly left without saying a word.

A few steps from the chapel was another taverna, more elaborate than the one at the halfway station, complete with an enclosed area for larger, more formal functions with a spectacular 360-degree panoramic view of Athens, Piraeus, the Saronic Gulf, the islands, and the mountains in the distance. I promised myself that I would bring my family here one day when my grandchildren are older, because it may help them understand their παπου's character better, and more important, so that they can develop a greater appreciation of their heritage.

The National Gardens and Panathenaic Stadium

I was a marathon runner in those days, and one morning, without knowing where I was headed, I ran from the Saint George Lycabettus Hotel and through the busy streets of Athens, avoiding cars along the route. Needless to say, I received a number of curious stares, perhaps because Athenians were not accustomed to seeing a runner coursing through the center of Athens. Miraculously, without being hit, I reached the National Gardens (Εθνηνικος Κυπος) and continued through a path surrounded by short olive trees. Abruptly, within a few hundred meters, the path ended, and I was standing on a precipice overlooking the Acropolis in the distance.

Directly below me, at the base of that precipice and wedged into the Athenian hillside, stood the impressive horseshoe-shaped Panathenaic Stadium (Παναθηωαικο Σταδιο). Built by Lycourgos in 300 BC, it is a spectacular structure with its marble gleaming in the bright morning sunlight. It is also known as Kallimarmaro (καλλιμαρμαρο), because it is the only stadium in the world built entirely of marble. It had been reconstructed from the remains of an ancient stadium, seats 50,000 spectators, hosted the first modern Olympic games, and was the finish line during the 2004 Olympic marathon.

High school and college track athletes and their coaches were running on its track, and being careful not to interfere with their workout, I stepped onto the track and continued my run. It was a most exhilarating and nostalgic experience to be running in the place where ancient Greek runners ran. The only thing I regret was that I was not presented with an olive wreath crown when I finished... perhaps the next time.

Mykonos

On that first trip to Greece, having completed a lecture, I decided to take a ferry from Pireaus to Mykonos to enjoy that island's traditions. The next morning, I was picked up at 5:00 a.m. by a taxi driver in a shiny Mercedes Benz. He steered a wild and dangerous course through the streets of Athens toward Pireaus. Miraculously, he dropped me off safely.

I secured a first-class passage, thinking I would have a tranquil six-hour ferry ride across the Aegean Sea to Mykonos, one of the islands in the Cyclades group. I should have known better; when you are with Greeks, the word *tranquility* does not exist. I arrived at the dock in Pireaus at 6:00 a.m., so I sat on a pylon and watched the stevedores and other workers prepare their ships for departure. Finally, at 7:00 a.m., I boarded the ferry named *Panagia Tinou* and discovered that the first-class section included approximately two hundred other passengers, which probably included everyone on the ferry, most of whom were chain-smoking cigarettes.

When I entered the first-class section, I was encouraged to see that it was equipped with a bar, until I realized that this bar did not serve alcoholic beverages. Alas, the only item on the menu was dry Greek cheese pie (τιροπιτα), which, by the way, is a typical breakfast item in Greece, but how much of that can you eat in six hours? The one element of particular interest, however, was that, despite being crammed into the first-class compartment, no one seemed to complain. Instead, I detected a sense of serenity, a satisfaction that my fellow passengers were on board and headed for a calm journey to the Cyclades. I smiled and thought, *How would this scenario be tolerated by*

IT IS THE WILL OF THE GODS: I'M COMING HOME, DAD

Americans? Perhaps we should adopt that Mediterranean philosophy regarding tranquility and happiness.

Nevertheless, after enduring that six-hour ferry ride from Pireaus to Mykonos, I quickly disembarked and was rapidly greeted by a cheerful driver who somehow knew my name, as well as how and when I was arriving. Even more astonishing, he had a fresh frappe (φραππε, γλικο) ready for me—another example of Grecian hospitality. We talked on the way to the hotel, and I asked him what his role was.

He calmly replied, "I'm the owner." I asked him why he, as the owner, would come to the harbor to pick me up, and he said, "Why not? We are Greeks, aren't we? That's what we do!"

Amazed, I responded, "Yes, after all, we are Greeks, and that's what we do!"

LATER, IN THE EVENING, BEFORE a colleague of mine was due to arrive on the island, I went into Mykonos town for dinner and decided on a small outdoor taverna in the harbor. I sat at a small wooden table covered by a red-and-white tablecloth with a small flickering candle. The table was separated from the water by a thirty-inch-high stone wall that provided me with a breathtaking view of the harbor as well as the cruise ships offshore, their lights twinkling softly like stars in the dark Aegean night. Other docked cruise liners preparing to embark for another island were retrieving their passengers, who were returning after a short excursion into Mykonos town. Above, the full, bright yellow Mediterranean moon bathed the harbor with golden light, and its reflection sparkled as it skipped over the waves that gently embraced the stone wall and provided adequate light for dinner. I kept a poster-sized picture of the incredibly spectacular postcard setting of that taverna and the harbor, and that picture is a constant reminder of my wonderful experience.

Initially, I ordered a glass of red wine and sat there contentedly enjoying the splendor and the serenity of the moment. Eventually, however, the warm glow prompted me to order dinner that included a peasant salad and fish. After completing dinner and two glasses of red wine, I asked the waiter for the check. In Greek restaurants, waiters will wait until you ask for the check before giving it to you, unlike most American restaurants, where you are practically ushered out the door as soon as you have completed your dinner. Well, the waiter came back within a few minutes, not with the check as I requested, but with a bottle of red wine, bread, and two glasses. Without hesitation, he pulled up a chair and asked me, "Why are you in a hurry? You are alone, and perhaps with no place to go this evening. If I am correct, we sit, and we drink wine. What could be more beautiful than this place?"

And he was right. What could be more beautiful than this place? It is this passion, this love for life, this hospitality that makes me proud to be a Greek. We sat for at least two hours, drinking wine, talking, followed by periods of silence, simply appreciating life. I thought of the contrast in philosophies and in the Mediterranean lifestyle. It's not so bad, is it? I know what Zorba would say: "The wine and the children speak the truth!"

Rhodes

Later, a Greek physician from Rhodes recommended that my colleagues and I should go to dinner and then to a specific nightclub on the beach close to our hotel for kefi. Of course, without hesitation we all agreed, but the non-Greeks in our group were unaware of Greek time. Dinner for Greeks, as you are aware, begins at approximately 10:00 p.m. Further, the non-Greeks were astonished to learn that the nightclub did not open until midnight. Nevertheless, in the spirit of unity and Hellenism, we all forged ahead with the plan. Dinner, as expected, was excellent, and those in our group who had become fatigued by the late hour following dinner were abruptly rejuvenated by the captivating music at the nightclub.

The music and dancing continued throughout the night and into the morning without intermission, and the non-Greeks in the group quickly developed a feel for the term "Greek time." Before long, we all became mesmerized by the music so that time had ultimately become a non-issue. I have a vivid recollection of my Italian colleague and closest friend dancing with his head and neck hyperextended, his eyes closed, and his arms extended as if they were controlled by the god's puppeteers, while flowers were tossed over his and the other dancers' heads. He had, without any question, attained kefi, and to the amazement of the non-Greeks who were with us, very little alcohol was consumed. The music was intoxicating enough!

We eventually wandered out of the nightclub at approximately 6:00 a.m. in what I am certain resembled a zombie apocalypse. Remarkably, behind us, the orchestra was still playing, and many of the patrons were still dancing. Our next stop was the hotel, where we put on our bathing suits for a quick plunge into the Mediterranean, followed by a shower, coffee, and breakfast (incidentally, cigarettes and coffee are considered by the Greeks to be the "breakfast of champions.") and then back to the symposium for the morning session. The remainder of that afternoon was spent recovering on the beach! "YASSOU!"

I HAVE NOT TAKEN MY family to Greece yet. I am waiting impatiently for my grandchildren to become older before beginning that epic odyssey so that they will appreciate elements of their heritage. I want my grandson, Gabe, to see Thermopylae, where Leonidas and the Spartans fought courageously, and my granddaughter, Alex, to visit the Oracle at Delphi on Mount Parnassus, the place where the priestess, the pythia, spoke for Apollo and uttered prophecies. I want them to visit the Chapel of Saint George, a symbol of Greek Orthodoxy, on the summit of Lycabettus, and the Parthenon standing above the walls of the Acropolis, symbolic of the strength of the Hellenic Republic. I want them to observe the changing of the guard at the Tomb of the Unknown Soldier at Syntagma and to marvel at the blue waters of the Saronic Gulf and the Aegean Sea. I want them to meet my friend Haralambros, have lunch at his taverna in the Plaka, and see the Greeks playing cards, drinking ouzo, and arguing. I want them to be in the place once occupied by Hippocrates, Homer, Plato, Socrates, Aristotle, Pythagoras, Achilles, Leonidas, and Kosmas. I want my family to feel my Greekness, to sense what it is like to be Greek, to understand my chaotic behavior and why I am happy that I am a Greek!

And when I arrive in Greece again, this time with my family, I can say to my dad, "I'm home again, Dad, and this time, look who I brought with me! Opa!"

Questions for Discussion

1. What are some of the common characteristics of Greekness? Can you name some similarities between your own culture and the Greek culture? How does your culture differ from the Greek culture?

2. How does the author's experience growing up in the Greek community when he was a child differ from the community where Greek youth grow up today? Do you think they have a similar experience? If not, why?

3. How important is the role of the family in the Greek community? What are some examples of this importance? What can we learn from the Greeks about family?

4. The author paints a vivid picture of the Greek communities—the agora. What are some of the particulars about this description that stood out in your mind? Can you draw any similarities between the Greek agora the author grew up in and the community where you grew up?

5. Discuss the importance of religion in the Greek way of life. Do you think religion has an influence over the decisions Greeks make in everyday life?

6. The author's description of religion and superstition presents an interesting dichotomy. Discuss the presence of superstition and how you think it sways their religious views.

7. Traditions are an important part of the Greek culture. How do you think assimilation has affected and will continue to affect these traditions? Can they be saved?
8. Discuss the Greek diet. Have you tried the foods that the author names? If not, would you?
9. Kefi is a common theme in the book. Have you ever experienced kefi? Maybe if it wasn't called kefi, it was called something else. Please discuss.
10. Discuss the important lessons that the Greek culture has to offer. Are there any of these in particular that you wish you could pass along to your own community?
11. Given the examples cited in this book regarding the use of the words chaos and passion, do you think that they represent qualities of Greekness?
12. Considering that many Greeks continue to utilize homeopathic medicine, what is your opinion regarding its efficacy as described in this book?
13. What is your opinion of talismans and the "evil eye"? Can you illustrate similar viewpoints within other ethnic groups and cultures regarding these superstitions?

Author Q&A

Q: What inspired you to write *Opa!*? Can you speak a bit about that and your aspirations for the book?

>**A:** The following quote is taken from Thetis, mother of Achilles, as she spoke to him before the start of the Trojan War. She said, "They want you to fight in Troy. If you stay in Larissa, you will find peace and you will find a wonderful woman. You will have sons and daughters and they will have children and they will love you, and when you are gone they will remember you. But when your children are dead and their children after them, your name will be lost." (*Troy*, written by David Benioff and directed by Wolfgang Petersen, 2004). My objective in writing *Opa!* is to leave something tangible about my life to my daughter, my grandchildren, and perhaps to their children as well.

Q: You describe a lot of heartwarming stories from your experience growing up as a Greek American. What was it like to revisit so many wonderful memories and experiences as you wrote this memoir?

A: It brought me back to those days of simplicity and security. It rekindled memories of wonderful experiences that I had while growing up in the agora. First-generation family members, extended family members, and friends, all with their unique personalities, many of which I have attempted to characterize in *Opa!*, filled my life with laughter. Although I am saddened that many of them are no longer with me, my memories of them, many of which I have shared with you, will continue to burn brightly within me. By having completed *Opa!*, I hope that my daughter and grandchildren will remember many of these experiences and traditions that are so important in my life.

Q: Can you share a little bit about your writing process? Do you have any writing rituals, for example?

A: My writing process can be described as chaotic at best. There were instances when I would glare at the computer and it would stare back at me, wondering if I was going to start writing! On rare occasions, I was able to write without effort. And of course, in those circumstances, I usually had time constraints. Finally, on multiple occasions, I would get a thought in the middle of the night that prevented me from falling asleep, and I would get up to write.

Q: How has growing up Greek shaped your view of the world?

A: Growing up Greek in the agora gave me a myopic perspective of the world, because to those of us who grew up there, the agora was our world. Many of us who left the agora and ventured into "the world" experienced a culture shock. Nonetheless, I began to realize that all people are more alike than they are different.

AUTHOR Q&A

Q: Do you maintain a Mediterranean diet? If so, what are some of the health benefits you enjoy because of that diet?

> **A:** I try to follow the Mediterranean diet despite my chaotic schedule. My evening meal generally consists of a Greek peasant salad with balsamic vinegar and extra virgin olive oil, bread, a piece of Kasseri cheese, and occasionally a piece of chicken or fish. I restrict my consumption of red meat to perhaps once or twice a month. I feel strongly that adherence to many aspects of the Mediterranean diet complemented by a consistent, moderate physical exercise protocol will reduce the risk of developing cardiovascular disease.

Q: You paint such a wonderful picture of your aunts and uncles and family throughout the book. What was it like growing up with such a large family?

> **A:** In few words—love and security. We were always surrounded by family and relatives who protected us, looked after our needs to the best of their abilities, and taught us respect. To the Greeks, the extended family and the nuclear family are synonymous.

Q: What are some of the ways the Greek culture has evolved since you were a child? These must include positive and negative changes. Can you talk a little bit about them both?

> **A:** Certain aspects of the Greek culture appear to have been either diluted or lost since I was a child. The extended family, for example, although still present, appears to be less cohesive. When I was young, my primary language was Greek. Despite being fluent in Greek at that time, I attended Greek school every afternoon to learn how to

read and write Greek and to learn about Greek history and culture. Although still present, Greek formal education and bilinguality appears to have decreased with succeeding generations.

Since many aspects of our daily lives were Greek, our interactions with other cultures inevitably were affected. This became more apparent as we became older and left the agora. We were more comfortable with Greeks and would look for them. When I went to college, I would read the Greek newspapers, look for the Greek clubs, Greek dances, the Greek Church, anywhere where I could find Greeks. I was constantly looking for people like me! This aspect of cultural isolation that developed while I was growing up in the agora had a profound negative effect on my ability to interact with non-Greeks. Initially, when I left the agora for college, I became a "Greek mariner, adrift at sea." Fortunately, it appears that this aspect of cultural isolation has decreased in succeeding generations as assimilation progresses. Moreover, I feel that cultural diversity is vital and that all ethnicities and races should retain their cultural identities.

Q: Did you have a favorite chapter to write in *Opa!*? If so, could you speak a bit on why it was your favorite?

A: One evening, during my daughter's pregnancy, I arrived at her apartment carrying a large cardboard box filled with food from the Greek club. As I began to climb the stairs to their apartment, my daughter and son-in-law sprinted past me, immediately followed by my wife, who hastily turned and blurted out, "Samantha's water broke!" Glued in my tracks and at a complete loss for words, I finally uttered, "What about this food?" Regaining my composure, I immediately put the box down on the stair, jumped into the car, and a few hours later became a proud grandfather to Alexsandria and Gabriel. It was

AUTHOR Q&A

a paramount event in my life! From the first moment when I cuddled them in the neonatal intensive care unit (NICU) to this day, I am ecstatic when I am with them.

The chapter on Greek superstition and homeopathic medicine was a second favorite. Although I had experience with both of these areas, the Greek Orthodox Church's position on the evil eye as compared to the intensity of the layman's beliefs intrigued me. Many aspects of homeopathic medicine, as well as the lay exoneration of the evil eye, remain viable within the Greek culture and are practiced today, especially by the older generation of Greeks. It remains a fascinating practice to me.

Q: Have you ever considered living in Greece permanently? Why or why not?

> **A:** No. Although I love the Greek people, enjoy visiting Greece frequently, and remain passionate regarding my Greekness, I am a Greek American, and the United States of America is my home.

Q: What is the one lesson you hope readers will take away from *Opa!*? And, more specifically, do you have any particular advice you'd like to offer future generations of Greek readers?

> **A:** To all my readers, I hope that you have enjoyed *Opa!* and remember that "even though we are all unique, we are the same!" To my young Greek readers: Be proud of your heritage, and celebrate your Greekness! And remember that "the blood of ancient Greek heroes runs through your veins!"

Glossary

αγορα, **agora**—a central gathering place, marketplace

αδης, **Hades**—Greek word for underworld

αποκριες, **apokries**—"goodbye to meat" (Carnival period that begins ten weeks before Greek Orthodox Easter and ends on the weekend before Clean Monday)

αρματoloi, **Armatoloi**—Greek insurgents, mountain fighters

Αθηνα, **Athena**—Goddess of war; city of Athens named after her

βασιλοπιτα, **vasilopita**—St. Basil bread or pie containing a hidden coin

βασκανια, **vaskania**—evil eye

βασκανος, **vaskanos**—envious person

βουζουκι, **bouzouki**—a Greek string musical instrument resembling a mandolin

γαμος απο συνοικεσιο—arranged marriage

γεια μας, **yia mas**—cheers, good health

γεια σου, γασσου, **yassou**—a greeting meaning "hello, to your good health"

γιαουρτι, **yiaourti**—yogurt

γλικο, **gliko**—sweet

ελευθερια, **eleutheria**—freedom

Επανασταση, **epanastasi**—Greek war of Independence against the Ottoman Empire, celebrated on March 25th

επανωκαλυμμαυχιον, **epanokalimavkion**—priest hat

επιταφιος, **epitaphios**—a large embroidered cloth bearing the image of Christ

ευζωνας, **evzone**—historical elite mountain infantryman; (cap) Greek Presidential Guard

θανατος, **Thanatos**—death

θανατος η ελευθερια, **"Eleftheria; Thanatos"**—freedom or death

θηρα, **thera**—ancient city on a ridge in Santorini

καλως ηλθατε, **kalos ilthate**—welcome

καφενειο, **kafenion**—Greek coffeehouse

κεφι, **kefi**—a sense of high spirit, relaxation

κλεφτης, **kleftis**—Greek mountain fighters

κομπολοι, **komboloi**—Greek worry beads

GLOSSARY

λουκανικο, **loukaniko**—Greek pork sausage, usually with leeks

μακαρια, **makaria**—internment meal

μονοπατι, **monopati**—footpath

μπακλαβα, **baklava**—a pastry with layers of phyllo, chopped nuts, and honey

ξεματιασμα, **xematiasma**—curing the evil eye

ξενος, **xenos**—a non-Greek, foreigner, stranger

οικογενεια, **oikogeneia**—family

οπα! **Opa!**—an emotional expression of enthusiasm

ορεκτικα, **orektika**—appetizers

ουζο, **ouzo**—anise-flavored aperitif; may be served with ice

παθος, **pathos**—to suffer, passion

παλικαρη, **palikari**—young Greek military man, lad, or youth

παπας, **papas**—priest

Παπου, **Papou**—grandfather

πλακα, **plaka**—old section of Athens, studded with shops and tavernas

Πλατεια Συνταγματος, **Syntagma Square**—central square in Athens (changing of the guard occurs at the Tomb of the Unknown Soldier at Syntagma Square)

πνευμα, **pneuma**—spirit

πρασα—leeks

ταβλι, **tavli**—Greek backgammon

τιροπιτα, **tiropita**—Greek cheese pie

τρισαγιον, **triasgion**—thrice holy (a hymn of the Divine Liturgy)

τσαρουχια, **tsarouhia**—red leather shoes with a black pom, worn by the Greek Palace Guard

τσιπουρα, **tsipoura**—porgy, a fatty white fish with a mild flavor and firm flakes; high in omega-3-fatty acids

τσολιαδες, **tsoliades**—Evzones, Presidential Guard

τσολιας, **tsolias**—evzone, "well belted"

φιλοξενια, **filoxenia**—a love for foreigners

φιλοτιμο, **filotimo**—the love of honor, respect

φουστανελλα, **foustanella**—traditional pleated skirt worn by the Evzones (a ceremonial uniform worn by the Greek Palace Guards)

φραππε, **frappe**—frappe

φραππε, **γλικο**—frappe, sweet

χορος, **xoros**—dance

χορτα, **xorta**—greens

χωριο, **xorio**—village

χωριατικη σαλατα, **xoriatiki salata**—peasant salad; tomatoes, onions, feta cheese, cucumbers, olives, oregano

ψυχη, **psixi**—soul

About the Author

DR. COSMAS RECEIVED HIS DEGREES from Boston University and the University of Massachusetts. He was awarded a scholarship and received a teaching fellowship at Boston University and a teaching/research fellowship at the University of Massachusetts. He served in the medical unit of the New Hampshire Air National Guard. He has been an instructor at Boston University and is currently an associate professor emeritus at the University of Connecticut, an adjunct professor at the University of Rhode Island, and a senior staff therapist at select medical sports medicine and outpatient rehabilitation clinics.

His research interests include the effects of subclinical hypothyroidism on heart and skeletal muscle, structural changes within the aging heart, physical activity as an age retardant, skeletal muscle metabolic and structural alterations as indicators of cardiovascular disease, and morphological alterations in the left ventricle during chronic sustained hypertension progressing to early heart failure. He has published numerous scientific articles and has addressed national and international audiences.

He played baseball at Boston University, has played semiprofessional baseball, has run many marathons, and has competed in several triathlons. He continues to practice physical therapy and sports medicine. He continues to run, bike, and swim and is a passionate proponent of physical activity as an age retardant. However, most important, he loves being a papou!

www.ingramcontent.com/pod-product-compliance
Lightning Source LLC
Chambersburg PA
CBHW020252030426
42336CB00010B/733